Stress, Affluence and Sustainable Consumption

T0353027

Why do affluent consumers almost automatically acquire new versions or variations of products already at their disposal? Even though most of us know that this novelty consumption poses a serious threat to an environmentally and socially sustainable future, we continue to do it. Why?

Research shows that consumption of new automobiles, clothing, furniture, electronics, home furnishing, household apparel, mobile phones, etc., is motivated by a desire to feel more secure, less anxious and better mood-wise. Affluent consumers seem to engage in novelty consumption not to feel better but rather to avoid feeling bad. *Stress, Affluence and Sustainable Consumption* discusses sustainable consumption from a stress perspective, adding an embodied understanding to the sustainability-related consumption challenges that we face today.

A stress perspective on affluent consumption differs from current understandings on consumption, as it fully acknowledges the consumer as having a body (including a mind) that reacts to the numerous product offerings and retail spaces, both physical and online. A stress perspective can explain how our bodies try to cope with an overload of perceptual input provided by advertising messages, product launches and even store structures.

This book will be of great interest to students and researchers of consumer psychology, sustainable consumption studies, sustainable marketing and markets as well as sustainable development more generally.

Cecilia Solér is Associate Professor in Marketing at the School of Business, Economics and Law, University of Gothenburg, Sweden.

Routledge Studies in Sustainability

For a full list of titles in this series, please visit www.routledge.com/Routledge-Studies-in-Sustainability/book-series/RSSTY

"Those concerned with sustainability and consumption have neglected the underlying compulsion to consume, and how it becomes a learned and habituated feature of contemporary life. This intriguing and provocative book sheds important new light on the stress of affluent consumption and the dysfunction that gives rise to it. This book is guaranteed to make you think again."

– Peter Wells, Professor of Business and Sustainability,
Cardiff Business School, UK

Stress, Affluence and Sustainable Consumption

Cecilia Solér

LONDON AND NEW YORK

First published 2018 by Routledge

2 Park Square, Milton Park, Abingdon, Oxfordshire OX14 4RN

52 Vanderbilt Avenue, New York, NY 10017

Routledge is an imprint of the Taylor & Francis Group, an informa business

First issued in paperback 2019

© 2018 Cecilia Solér

The right of Cecilia Solér to be identified as author of this work
has been asserted by her in accordance with sections 77 and 78 of
the Copyright, Designs and Patents Act 1988.

All rights reserved. No part of this book may be reprinted
or reproduced or utilised in any form or by any electronic,
mechanical, or other means, now known or hereafter invented,
including photocopying and recording, or in any information
storage or retrieval system, without permission in writing from the
publishers.

Trademark notice: Product or corporate names may be trademarks
or registered trademarks, and are used only for identification and
explanation without intent to infringe.

British Library Cataloguing-in-Publication Data
A catalogue record for this book is available from the British Library

Library of Congress Cataloging-in-Publication Data
A catalog record for this book has been requested

ISBN: 978-1-138-04075-5 (hbk)
ISBN: 978-0-367-24802-4 (pbk)

Typeset in Times New Roman
by Apex CoVantage, LLC

Contents

Figures

Acknowledgements

Chronic stress has been a part of my life for many years, as is the case for many affluent Swedish women and men trying to manage both family and career. My own experience of chronic stress and that of others have been the source of inspiration for this book. I have had the opportunity to learn from very knowledgeable people how stress reactions affect the brain and the body. In particular I would like to thank Gunilla Wengholm, Lisbeth Währborg and Josef Abadi for their wisdom and care. In addition, I have found great inspiration in books written by Peter Währborg, Aleksander Perski and Giorgio Grossi. My colleagues at the School of Business, Economics and Law at Gothenburg University have contributed with constructive comments at various stages of my research on consumption and stress. Thank you as well to Diane Martin, Frank Lindberg, Lena Mossberg, Benjamin Hartmann, Peter Zackariasson and Dannie Kjellegaard. To my beloved children and husband – thank you for putting up with all this writing. This book is dedicated to you.

Gothenburg, June 4, 2017

Part 1

Overview

Stress and affluent sustainable
consumption

1 Introduction

The sustainability of affluent consumption

This book addresses affluent sustainable consumption from an embodied perspective. It focuses on the increasing levels of affluent consumption that follow increases in current household income and which pose a serious threat to the achievement of an environmentally sustainable system of consumption and production (Alfredsson, 2004; Baxter and Jermann, 1999; Brännlund et al., 2007; Carlsson-Kanyama et al., 2005; Lusardi, 1996; Hurth, 2010; Lenzen et al., 2006; Tukker et al., 2010). All consumption activities have not only an impact on the environment through resource and energy use, but also threaten planetary boundaries (Rockström et al., 2009). The concept of planetary boundaries suggests nine earth system related to global production and consumption processes – climate change; biodiversity loss, the nitrogen cycle, the phosphorus cycle, stratospheric ozone depletion, ocean acidification, global freshwater use, land use change, atmospheric aerosol loading and chemical pollution – that potentially risks being disrupted (Biermann et al., 2012; Rockström et al., 2009). The concept of tipping points is used to denote the threshold value that should not be passed if we want to avoid disruptive earth systems. Rockström et al. (2009) estimate that the threshold values of three earth boundary conditions highly connected to global provisioning and exchange systems – climate change, biodiversity loss and the nitrogen cycle – have already been surpassed. Thus, in a resource-constrained world, in which consumption levels need to be increased for reasons of poverty and equality in developing economies, it is urgent to reduce the level of consumption by the affluent (Cohen et al., 2010). World Bank statistics presented in Figure 1.1 show that (1) high income households increase their consumption expenditures at a higher rate than lower income households over time and (2) OECD high income households increase their consumption faster than non-OECD high income households.

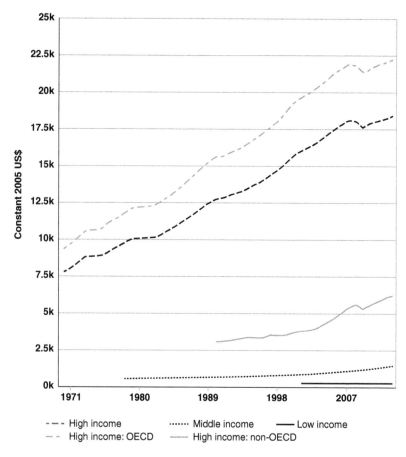

Figure 1.1 Household expenditure per capita in relationship to income, 1971–2007
Source: The World Bank, 2017, Global Consumption Database

Defining affluent consumption

Affluent consumers carry a disproportionate share of the environmental impact of market exchanges, as illustrated by the planetary boundary concept. Therefore, it is important to define affluent consumption as well as the environmental impact that follows from it. By doing so, we can differentiate between affluent consumption and consumption "experienced by the people of poverty and adequacy" (Sheehan, 2010). Affluent consumption is characteristic of Western economies, but growing numbers of affluent consumers are found in developing economies such as China and India, their numbers rising as incomes increase.

Affluent consumption is enabled by financial resources, which are accessed by systems of credit to varying degrees (Cohen, 2007; Ransome, 2005). In this book, affluent consumption is defined in relative terms rather than as a set of fixed resources or in terms of the ownership of specific goods. The relative definition of Western affluent consumption is based on two inter-twined dimensions: access to resources for consumption purposes and consumption objects as symbols for social desirability. These two dimensions of affluent consumption are interdependent, as surplus income is needed to consume beyond basic needs. Access to surplus income creates the capacity to freely spend and choose which products and services to consume, as well as the expectation of being able to do so (Ransome, 2005). In accordance with the affluence hypothesis, the consumer cultures of the industrialized West, and our identities, feelings and way of living, are to a large degree shaped by consumption (Arnould and Thompson, 2005; Campbell, 1987; Ransome, 2005). Readily accessible surplus income means that affluent consumers not only can choose what to consume, but also can consume products and services for reasons of "pleasure and satisfaction in and of themselves without always being tied to satisfaction of basic needs" (Ransome, 2005, p. 5).

One consequence of the affluence hypothesis is that the predominant driver for affluent spending is the desire to acquire novel and socially desirable products and services. Novelty is a generic quality in so called fashion-driven industries in which products are subject to frequent updates in style and design. Marketing and advertising practices, where new products are linked to idealized identities, heavily support "the social pressure" (keeping up with the Outer and Inner Joneses) to acquire products and services in fashion (Cohen, 2007; Moisander et al., 2010). Automobiles, clothing, furniture, electronics, home furnishing, household apparel, mobile phones, clothing and holiday destinations are examples of products that are continuously subject to change, obsolescence or replacement, and are forcefully advertised as an essential part of happy and successful lives (Desmeules, 2002; Moisander et al., 2010). The fashionable character of products and services resides not in their inherent functional qualities but in their social value (Banister and Hogg, 2004; Bourdieu, 1984; Rafferty, 2011; Schiermer, 2011; Simmel, 1904; Thompson and Haytko, 1997). They are consumed to a substantial extent because they feature novel characteristics that are valued by others, although their functionalities often partially reside in the pre-existing object (Alvesson, 2013). As novel products are socially desired and highly valued in Western consumer cultures, refraining from consuming these can be problematic for individual consumers. Research shows that fashion consumption is motivated by insecurity alleviation and mood restoration (Burroughs and Rindfleisch, 2002; Clarke and Miller, 2002; Dittmar, 2008; Mick and Demoss, 1990; Moschis, 2007; Pavia and Mason, 2004; Woodruffe-Burton and Elliott, 2005). Thus, it seems that affluent consumers continuously engaged in increasing consumption – which is unsustainable – do so not to feel good about themselves or to enjoy life but rather to avoid feeling bad about not having the latest products or visited the newest exotic holiday destination.

In this book, affluent consumption in the Western consumer culture context is defined as *the financial possibility to consume in accordance with socially desirable consumption (fashion) trends*. This does not mean that all affluent consumers "overconsume", i.e. engage in consumption of goods and services just for the sake of socially desirable novelty. Instead, this definition of affluent consumption acknowledges that such consumption comes in various shades depending on financial resources as well as interest and engagement in the marketplace.

Affluence and unsustainable consumption

One way to show the environmental impact of affluent consumption (in relation to the earth's capacity to provide resources needed without exceeding planetary boundaries) is to use ecological footprint analysis (Cohen, 2007; Wackernagel et al., 1999). The ecological footprint is a tool that estimates the productive land needed to uphold and sustain resources for consumption and waste assimilation of a specific population (Wackernagel et al., 1999). The concept of the earth's carrying capacity, or biocapacity, is used to illustrate "human demand on the environment into the area required for the production of food and other goods, together with the absorption of wastes" (Wackernagel et al., 2002, p. 9266). The biocapacity depends on land type and the productive capacity of the land (Global Footprint Network, 2016). If we assume generational equality and solidarity, and if we desire to live within the capacity of our planet, the current biocapacity per person is 1.7 global hectares (Global Footprint Network, 2016). In other words, we have 1.7 hectares each at our disposal to assure that our needs are met. If our way of living requires more than 1.7 hectares, someone else's ability to live within the earth's carrying capacity and planetary boundaries is at risk. For example, if a nation's ecological footprint per capita is 6.8 hectares, the citizens' way of living in this country requires almost four times the resources and wastes that our planet can reproduce and absorb.

Current ecological footprint data show that all affluent Western economies, as well as a large group of developing economies, demand many more resources and waste than can be regenerated and absorbed by planet Earth. More specifically, the ecological footprint per capita in global hectares – i.e. a nation's total ecological footprint divided by the total population of the nation for a full list, see www.footprintnetwork.org/resources/data/ – are: Luxemburg 15.8; Australia 9.3; USA/Canada 8.2; Singapore 8; Belgium 7.4; Sweden 7.3; Oman 7.5; Estonia 6.9; Latvia 6.3; Israel 6.2; Austria 6.1; Mongolia 6.1; Finland 5.9; South Korea and Russia 5.7; New Zealand/ Ireland 5.6; Japan/Norway 5; Botswana/Montenegro 3.8; Malaysia/Spain 3.7; China 3.4; South Africa 3.3; and Brazil 3. These examples illustrate the predominance of unsustainable consumption in countries where a majority of consumers are assumed to be affluent, in terms of having access to surplus income that makes it possible for them to consume in accordance with socially desirable consumption trends. However, the high ecological footprint of countries like Mongolia, with a relatively very low BNP per capita, illustrates that the biocapacity of the productive land and waste assimilation (Mongolia depends heavily on its mining industry, which produce waste) has a great impact on footprint analysis.

In sum, the ecological footprint analysis illustrates affluent consumption as intimately related to an ecological deficit which can be characterized as "importing biocapacity through trade, liquidating national ecological assets or emitting carbon dioxide waste into the atmosphere" (Global Footprint Network, 2016).

What unsustainable consumption, then, is characteristic of Western affluence? As mentioned earlier, not all affluent consumers consume in an unsustainable manner, even though they have the financial means to do so. However, large groups of affluent consumers do engage in highly unsustainable consumption practices that require large inputs of resources and energy. Brendan Sheehan (2010) describes in *The Economics of Abundance* the characteristics of an average affluent household: owned or rented decent accommodation; multiple cars, televisions, mobile phones, computers, washrooms and bedrooms; holidays abroad and credit cards; buying new, fashionable clothing each season; different meals every day and occasional meals out; fitted kitchen with fridge, dish washer, washing machine and freezer; plentiful supply and variety of children's things, such as food, toys, clothes and electronic equipment; regular redecoration of the home and buying of a new car, personal grooming stuff, handbags, gadgets etc.; spending much of their leisure time shopping.

What this account does not tell us is that affluent consumption also demonstrates a tendency to acquire bigger residences, longer and more frequent holiday trips by plane, and more cars, mobile phones, computers, household apparel, sports equipment, furniture, clothes etc. (GfK, 2016; Statista,

2016). Thus, we as affluent consumers seem to be constantly engaged in the acquisition of products or variations of products already at our disposal. This means that affluent consumption not only reflects ownership of an increasing number of products, square meters and kilometres travelled per household but also a constant renewal of objects acquired and destinations. European consumers mainly spend their increased income on services, travelling and recreational activities rather than on increased retail consumption (GfK, 2016). Swedish consumers' expenditures increased by 23% 2004–2014, the greatest increases within the categories of furniture, interior design and maintenance (+57%), consumption abroad (+56%), personal communication (+50%) and recreational activities (+48%) (Konsumtionsrapporten, 2016). Consumer expenditure statistics can be translated into physical consumption. Swedish sales of private cars increased between 2001 and 2015 by 18%, which corresponds to 470 private cars per thousand inhabitants (Statistics Sweden, 2017). In 2015, Swedish consumers used an average of 3.4 connected electronic devices (Statista, 2016). Recent statistics show that Swedes buy on average 13 kilos of textiles (clothes and textiles for the home) per person per year. This represents consumption of approximately 50 pieces of clothing per person per year. Swedes like to wear new clothes. They throw away 7.5 kilos of textiles per person yearly, and 60% of this waste is made up of textiles that are not worn down or ragged, i.e. perfectly usable and quite new clothes are thrown away (Swedish Environmental Protection Agency, 2017).

In the UK, retail sales 2014–2016 increased approximately 3% yearly (Government of the United Kingdom, 2016). Each year in the UK 44 billion pounds are spent on clothes consumption, representing 4,000 pounds' worth of an average British household (WRAP, 2016). The consumption of clothing has increased by 20% 2008–2015 (OECD, 2017). Approximately 30% of the clothes in British wardrobes have not been used the last year; 140 million pounds' worth of clothing goes to landfill each year, and in 2013 the UK exported used clothing for more than 380 million pounds (United Nations ComTrade, 2016). The increase in UK consumption of furnishings, household equipment and routine maintenance of the house was 17% 2008–2015 (OECD, 2017). UK consumers used an average of 3.4 connected electronic devices in 2015 (Statista, 2016). The latest statistics on private car ownership show that the number of cars in the UK increased by 1.6 million between 2011 and 2015 (Government of the United Kingdom, 2016).

The equivalent statistics for the US and Japan show car ownership per thousand inhabitants of 808 (the US) and 455 (Japan) (US Department of Energy, 2017). Consumer spending in the US increased by 1 % 2008–2016 (Trading Economics, 2017). US consumer spending on apparel increased by

15% between 2013 and 2015 (US Bureau of Labor Statistics, 2016), while Japan saw an increase of 9% between 2008 and 2014 in apparel consumption, 55% in furnishings, household equipment and routine maintenance of the house and 31% in recreation and culture, including consumer mobile devices (OECD, 2017). US consumers used an average of 3.9 connected electronic devices in 2015 (Statista, 2016).

Climate gas emissions and affluent consumption

Increasing affluent household consumption entails larger emissions of greenhouse gases. In the Swedish context, affluent consumers have a much higher climate impact than low-income consumers (Bolin et al., 2013). Per-person greenhouse gas emissions amount to ten tons of CO_2 per year for affluent Swedes, whereas the average Swede accounts for 7.5 tons of CO_2 emissions per year (Bolin et al., 2013). In the UK, the richest 10% of households emit three times that of the poorest 10% from energy use in the home and personal travel (Joseph RownTree Foundation, 2016). For the US, there is equally a large difference in the share of indirect carbon emissions between high and low income households (Shammin and Bullard, 2009).

Figure 1.2 illustrates the relationship between CO_2 emissions and income on a global level.

Affluent unsustainable consumption from an embodied stress perspective

From a sustainable consumption perspective, it is important to construct theoretical frameworks that explain the growth in affluent consumption (Wilk, 2002; Röpke, 2009). In consumption research, various theoretical perspectives have been applied to explain why increasingly affluent consumers are engaged in seemingly automatic consumption. After all, additional income could just as well be put in a savings account or used to make room for less work and more leisure time (Linder,1970; Sanne, 2002). As Richard Wilk (2011) notes,

> it is one of the great failures of social science in the last fifty years that we still do not know why some people seem to be happy with a stable level of consumer culture and others get on an endless cycle where wants become needs, and every new acquisition or activity just requires more consumption, in an endless upward spiral.
>
> (p. 46)

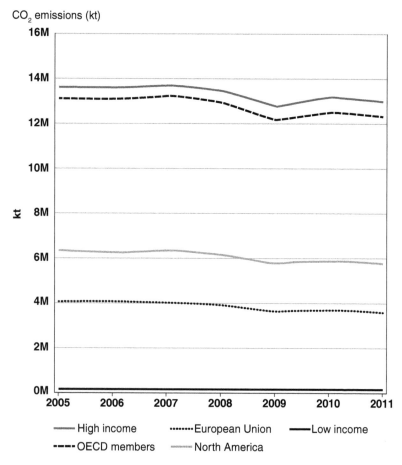

Figure 1.2 Relationship between CO_2 emissions and income, 2005–2011
Source: The World Bank, Global Consumption Database

Various theoretical schools of thought represented within the field of sustainable consumption have, to differing degrees, been used to understand rising affluent consumption. Cognitive-based studies deal with individual adoption of sustainable consumption patterns such as general awareness of climate change and espoused green values, an approach that has been labelled the attitude-behaviour gap (Young and Middlemiss, 2012; Stern, 2000), the knowledge-to-action gap (Markkula and Moisander, 2012) or the value-action gap (Shove, 2010; Steg, 2015). To a limited degree, these cognitive studies explain increasing affluent consumption through constructs such as attitudes, knowledge and values. The cultural perspective on sustainable consumption is primarily concerned with consumers' perceptions of sustainable consumption as part of identity-making (Autio et al., 2009; Cherrier et al., 2012), how they identify with environmental issues in everyday practices (Connolly and Prothero, 2008) and anti-consumption as reduction, reuse and rejection within cultures of consumption (Cherrier, 2009). This stream of culturally informed sustainable consumption research identifies the contradictory role of consumption objects as identity markers in a sustainable context. How can we expect (affluent) consumers to refrain from consuming objects that symbolize important parts of themselves (which is the true essence of consumer culture; see Arnould and Thompson, 2005) for the purpose of sustainable development? The consumer body is downplayed in these dominant mind-focused understandings – cognitive-based as well as culturally informed studies of sustainable consumption.

The recent practice turn within sustainable consumption studies recognizes the significant role of routine in (affluent) consumption practice (Geels et al., 2015), which is configured by elements of materiality, meaning and competence or equipment, images and skills (McMeekin and Southerton, 2007; Röpke, 2009; Shove et al., 2012). In practice-oriented studies on sustainable consumption, material elements are regarded as essential for the production of sustainable social practices (Preda, 1999; Schatzki, 2001; Spaargaren, 2011; Shove, 2010). Even though the human body is recognized as one aspect of the material elements that configure social practices, the consumer body is not explicitly addressed. In sum, the consumer body is downplayed in sustainable consumption research. The embodied stress perspective presented in this book adds a bodily dimension to the study of affluent consumption from a sustainable perspective.

Stress results from a situation that individuals perceive "as taxing or exceeding his or her resources and endangering his or her wellbeing" (Lazarus and Folkman, 1984, p. 19). In the consumption context, stress is defined as marketplace-induced environmental, social/internal or structural stressors that require the consumer to adjust his or her behaviour or cognition to maintain emotional and psychological control. In other words, the consumer must engage in stress-coping behaviour (Lazarus and Folkman, 1984; Moschis, 2007; Sapolsky, 2004; Thoits, 1995). A stress-theory framework thus situates the consumer body (which includes the mind) in the marketplace. This framework helps us conceptually to propose and discuss ways to understand and reduce affluent consumption through alternative consumer stress-coping strategies and changes in marketplace design. The causes and consequences of stress related to affluent consumption are the focus of later chapters in this book. The aim of the book is to (1) describe affluent consumption practice that is stress-induced, (2) describe how affluent consumption practice is stress reducing, and how consumption-related stress creates a vicious circle of stress and coping and (3) to discuss how affluent sustainable consumption can be promoted. The book recognizes that not all affluent consumption practices are stress-related, but focuses on affluent consumption practices where prior research indicates that a stress understanding is instrumental for making such consumption more sustainable. One important argument in this book is that affluent consumption practice, to some extent, counterbalances marketplace-induced stress linked to the continuous supply of novel products in the marketplace.

In Chapter 2, literature on sustainable consumption is reviewed from an embodied perspective, and the philosophical base for an embodied understanding of affluent consumption is outlined. From an embodied perspective, consumers' experience of the marketplace and its representations is a learned bodily activity and skill (Merleau-Ponty, 1962; Yakhlef, 2015). This relational view of consumer experience is explained through Gibson's concept of affordances (Gibson, 1979), which sheds light on how the consumer body responds to the solicitations of the marketplace and how affluent consumption practice reflects embodied learned dispositions (Dreyfus, 2002). Phenomenologically, taking the relational view between consumer and the marketplace even further, affluent consumption is described not as motivated by certain mental constructs, i.e. as primarily goal-directed, but rather as something that should be viewed as an adjustment to the affluent consumer life-world (Yakhlef, 2015). In Chapter 3, the embodied perspective on affluent consumption is related to sociological stress theory. The embodiment of consumption practice implies a coordinating function of the brain (allostatic thinking); stressors are assessed by the brain, which reacts to restore bodily balance when confronted by strains that threaten balance in the body and mind (Sterling and Eyer, 1988). More specifically, this chapter outlines affluent consumer role strains in terms of chronic affluent consumer stress in a consumer culture context as well as consumer stress coping, i.e. efforts to restore bodily balance that follow from a marketplace stressor-induced disequilibrium (Lazarus and Folkman, 1984; Moschis, 2007; Pearlin, 1983). To a large degree, the impact on an individual consumer of stressors in the marketplace depends on consumer coping strategies and stress mediators. In Chapter 3, alternative coping strategies, including active coping oriented toward modifying the stressor and avoidance coping that aims to reduce the tension caused by the stressor (Lazarus and Folkman, 1984; Sapolsky, 2004; Thoits, 1995), are elaborated on in the affluent consumption context. The most important stress mediators in an affluent consumption setting are stressors' potential threats to cultural/social values and consumers' ability to control and predict them (Moschis, 2007; Pearlin, 1989; Sapolsky, 2004).

In the second part of the book, affluent consumption-related stressors are described and discussed. In Chapter 4, environmental marketplace stressors related to "too much perceptual input" exceeding consumers' perceptual capacity (Chen et al., 2009; Lee, and Lee, 2004; Eppler and Mengis, 2004; Jacoby et al., 1974; Malhotra, 1982; Moschis, 2007) are presented as chronic affluent consumer overload. Perceptual overload is connected to consumers' sensory experiences in the marketplace (Bawden and Robinson, 2009; Jacoby et al., 1974; Malhotra, 1982) and to opportunities to use marketplace-mediated experiences, i.e. consumers' ability to experience media-dependent accounts of product offerings distant in space and time (Bawden and Robinson, 2009; Elliott, 2004). In Chapter 5, social and internalized marketplace-induced stressors are described in terms of "idealized identity" overload, characterized by think ideal – feel bad sequences (Dittmar, 2008; Halliwell and Dittmar, 2004; Halliwell et al., 2007) and consumption as compensation (Woodruffe-Burton and Elliott, 2005). Examples are drawn from fashion industries, where the novel fashion object is primarily valued because it is new and socially desirable and not because of its functionality (e.g. new models/variations of mobile phones, clothes, furniture, holiday trips etc.). So-called stress mediators (Moschis, 2007; Pearlin, 1989; Sapolsky, 2004) can explain why social/internalized marketplace-induced stressors can be perceived differently by individual consumers. The mediating capacity of perceived control and perceived threats to cultural and social values are discussed. Chapter 6 outlines structural affluent consumer life-style stressors. The relationship between "work/consumption rich, time poor" affluent consumers and stress is discussed. Links between affluent consumer subjective well-being and time spent working vs spent with family/friends (Kallis et al., 2013; Nässén and Larsson, 2015; Schor, 2005) are described from a stress perspective with implications on CO_2 emissions, and materialism is discussed as an affluent consumer trait.

Part 3 of the book deals with stress coping in the affluent consumption context. In Chapter 7, alternative consumer stress coping strategies are presented. An embodied reading of the insecurity and mood-alleviating properties of affluent fashion consumption practice (Burroughs and Rindfleisch, 2002; Clarke and Miller, 2002; Dittmar, 2008; Mick and Demoss, 1990; Moschis, 2007; O'Guinn and Faber, 1991; Pavia and Mason, 2004; Woodruffe-Burton and Elliott, 2005) suggests an understanding of such consumption practice as stress coping. From a stress perspective, the reliance on expert systems such as advertising, brands, peers or aesthetic experts to decide what products to choose is an example of a consumer support-seeking stress coping strategy (Duhachek, 2005; Sujan et al., 1999). Chapter 8 discusses possible sustainable consumption outcomes related to different consumer stress-coping strategies and Chapter 9 connects stress coping to consumer well-being. In Chapter 10, the embodied perspective on affluent consumption practice is linked to the socio-material marketplace.

Bibliography

Alfredsson, E.C. (2004), 'Green' consumption – No solution for climate change. *Energy*, Vol. 29 No. 4, pp. 513–24.

Alvesson, M. (2013), *The Triumph of Emptiness: Consumption, Higher Education, and Work Organization*, Oxford University Press, Oxford.

Arnould, E.J., and Thompson, C.J. (2005), Consumer Culture Theory (CCT): Twenty years of research. *Journal of Consumer Research*, Vol. 31 No. 4, pp. 868–82.

Autio, M., Heiskanen, E., and Heinonen, V. (2009), Narratives of 'green' consumers – The antihero, the environmental hero and the anarchist. *Journal of Consumer Behaviour*, Vol. 8 No. 1, pp. 40–53.

Banister, E.N., and Hogg, M.K. (2004), Negative symbolic consumption and consumers' drive for self-esteem: The case of the fashion industry. *European Journal of Marketing*, Vol. 38 No. 7, pp. 850–68.

Bawden, D., and Robinson, L. (2009), The dark side of information: Overload, anxiety and other paradoxes and pathologies. *Journal of Information Science*, Vol. 35 No. 2, pp. 180–91.

Baxter, M., and Jermann, U.J. (1999), *Household Production and the Excess Sensitivity of Consumption to Current Income*, National Bureau of Economic Research (No. w7046).

Belk, R., Ger, G., and Askegaard, S. (2003), The fire of desire: A multisited inquiry into consumer passion. *Journal of Consumer Research*, Vol. 30 No. 3, pp. 326–51.

Biermann, F., Abbott, K., Andresen, S., Bäckstrand, K., Bernstein, S., Betsill, M.M., . . . and Gupta, A. (2012), Navigating the Anthropocene: Improving earth system governance. *Science*, Vol. 335 No. 6074, pp. 1306–7.

Bolin, L., Larsson, J., Sinclair, R., Hellström, P., Palmestål, K., Svensson, I., and Mattson, B. (2013), *Klimatomställning Göteborg – Tekniska möjligheter och livsstilsförändringar*, Mistra Urban Futures Report 2013:5.

Bourdieu, P. (1984), *A Social Critique of the Judgement of Taste*, Routledge, London.

Brännlund, R., Ghalwash, T., and Nordström, J. (2007), Increased energy efficiency and the rebound effect: Effects on consumption and emissions. *Energy Economics*, Vol. 29 No. 1, pp. 1–17.

Burroughs, J.E., and Rindfleisch, A. (2002), Materialism and well-being: A conflicting values perspective. *Journal of Consumer Research*, Vol. 29 No. 3, pp. 348–70.

Campbell, C. (1987), *The Romantic Ethic and the Spirit of Modern Consumerism*, Blackwell, London.

Carlsson-Kanyama, A., Engström, R., and Kok, R. (2005), Indirect and direct energy requirements of city households in Sweden: Options for reduction, lessons from modeling. *Journal of Industrial Ecology*, Vol. 9 No. 1–2, pp. 221–35.

Chen, Y.C., Shang, R.A., and Kao, C.Y. (2009), The effects of information overload on consumers' subjective state towards buying decision in the internet shopping environment. *Electronic Commerce Research and Applications*, Vol. 8 No. 1, pp. 48–58.

Cherrier, H. (2009), Anti-consumption discourses and consumer-resistant identities. *Journal of Business Research*, Vol. 62 No. 2, pp. 181–190.

Cherrier, H., Szuba, M., and Özcaglar-Toulouse, N. (2012), Barriers to downward carbon emission: Exploring sustainable consumption in face of the glass floor. *Journal of Marketing Management*, Vol. 28 No. 3–4, pp. 397–419.

Chrousos, G.P., and Gold, P.W. (1992), The concepts of stress and stress system disorders: Overview of physical and behavioral homeostasis. *Journal of the American Medical Association*, Vol. 267 No. 9, pp. 1244–52.

Clarke, A., and Miller, D. (2002), Fashion and anxiety. *Fashion Theory*, Vol. 6 No. 2, pp. 191–214.

Cohen, M.J. (2007), Consumer credit, household financial management, and sustainable consumption. *International Journal of Consumer Studies*, Vol. 31 No. 1, pp. 57–65.

Cohen, M.J., Brown, H.S., and Vergragt, P.J. (2010), Individual consumption and systemic societal transformation: Introduction to the special issue. *Sustainability: Science, Practice, & Policy*, Vol. 6 No. 2.

Connolly, J., and Prothero, A. (2008), Green consumption: Life-politics, risk and contradictions. *Journal of Consumer Culture*, Vol. 8 No. 1, pp. 117–45.

Desmeules, R. (2002), The impact of variety on consumer happiness: Marketing and the tyranny of freedom. *Academy of Marketing Science Review*, Vol. 12, p. 1.

Dittmar, H. (2008), *Consumer Culture, Identity and Well-Being*, Psychology Press, New York.

Dreyfus, H.L. (2002), Intelligence without representation – Merleau-Ponty's critique of mental representation the relevance of phenomenology to scientific explanation. *Phenomenology and the Cognitive Sciences*, Vol. 1 No. 4, pp. 367–83.

Duhachek, A. (2005), Coping: A multidimensional, hierarchical framework of responses to stressful consumption episodes. *Journal of Consumer Research*, Vol. 32 No. 1, pp. 41–53.

Elliott, R. (2004), "Making up people: Consumption as a symbolic vocabulary for the construction of identity", in Ekström, K. and Brembek, H. (eds.), *Elusive Consumption*, Berg Publishers, Oxford, pp. 11–25.

Eppler, M.J., and Mengis, J. (2004), The concept of information overload: A review of literature from organization science, accounting, marketing, MIS, and related disciplines. *The Information Society*, Vol. 20 No. 5, pp. 325–44.

Frank, R.H. (2001), *Luxury Fever: Why Money Fails to Satisfy in an Era of Excess*, New York: Simon and Schuster.

Gallagher, S. (2005), *How the Body Shapes the Mind*, Oxford University Press, New York.

Geels, F.W., McMeekin, A., Mylan, J., and Southerton, D. (2015), A critical appraisal of sustainable consumption and production research: The reformist, revolutionary and reconfiguration positions. *Global Environmental Change*, Vol. 34, pp. 1–12.

GfK. (2016), European retail in 2016: Slow but real-value growth, www.gfk.com/insights/press-release/european-retail-in-2016/

Gibson, J.J. (1979), "The theory of affordances", in *The Ecological Approach to Visual Perception*, Houghton Mifflin Harcourt, Hopewell, pp. 56–60.

Global Footprint Network. (2016), Data and methodology, www.footprintnetwork.org/resources/data/, accessed March 27, 2017.

Government of the United Kingdom (2016), https://www.ons.gov.uk/business industryandtrade/retailindustry/bulletins/retailsales/previousReleases

Halliwell, E., and Dittmar, H. (2004), Does size matter? The impact of model's body size on advertising effectiveness and women's body-focused anxiety. *Journal of Social and Clinical Psychology*, Vol. 23 No. 1, pp. 104–22.

Halliwell, E., Dittmar, H., and Orsborn, A. (2007), The effects of exposure to muscular male models among men: Exploring the moderating role of gym use and
exercise motivation. *Body Image*, Vol. 4 No. 3, pp. 278–87.

Holmes, T.H., and Rahe, R.H. (1967), The social readjustment rating scale. *Journal
of Psychosomatic Research*, Vol. 11 No. 2, pp. 213–8.

Hurth, V. (2010), Creating sustainable identities: The significance of the financially
affluent self. *Sustainable Development*, Vol. 18 No. 3, pp. 123–34.

Jacoby, J., Speller, D.E., and Kohn, C.A. (1974), Brand choice behavior as a function of information load. *Journal of Marketing Research*, Vol. 11 No. 1, pp. 63–9.

Joseph RownTree Foundation (2016), https://www.jrf.org.uk/search?query=climate+
change&=

Kallis, G., Kalush, M., O'Flynn, H., Rossiter, J., and Ashford, N. (2013), 'Friday
off': Reducing working hours in Europe. *Sustainability*, Vol. 5 No. 4, pp. 1545–67.

Konsumtionsrapporten. (2016), GRI and CFK move in together, *Centrum för Kon-
sumtionsvetenskap*, http://cfk.gu.se/.

Lazarus, R.S., and Folkman, S. (1984), *Stress, Appraisal, and Coping*, Springer
Publishing Company, New York.

Lee, B.-K., and Lee, W.-N. (2004), The effect of information overload on consumer
choice quality in an on-line environment. *Psychology and Marketing*, Vol. 21
No. 3, pp. 159–83.

Lenzen, M., Wier, M., Cohen, C., Hayami, H., Pachauri, S., and Schaeffer, R. (2006),
A comparative multivariate analysis of household energy requirements in Australia, Brazil, Denmark, India and Japan. *Energy*, Vol. 31 No. 2–3, pp. 181–207.

Linder, S.B. (1970), *The Harried Leisure Class*, Columbia University Press, New
York, p. 135.

Lusardi, A. (1996), Permanent income, current income, and consumption: Evidence
from two panel data sets. *Journal of Business & Economic Statistics*, Vol. 14
No. 1, pp. 81–90.

Magaudda, P. (2011), When materiality 'bites back': Digital music consumption
practices in the age of dematerialization. *Journal of Consumer Culture*, Vol. 11
No. 1, pp. 15–36.

Malhotra, N.K. (1982), Information load and consumer decision making. *Journal of
Consumer Research*, Vol. 8 No. 4, pp. 419–30.

Markkula, A., and Moisander, J. (2012), Discursive confusion over sustainable consumption: A discursive perspective on the perplexity of marketplace knowledge.
Journal of Consumer Policy, Vol. 35 No. 1, pp. 105–25.

McMeekin, A., and Southerton, D. (2007), *Innovation and Final Consumption:
Social Practices, Instituted Modes of Provision and Intermediation*, CRIC Discussion Papers, University of Manchester, Manchester.

Merleau-Ponty, M. (1962), *Phenomenology of Perception*, Routledge, London.

Mick, D.G., and Demoss, M. (1990), Self-gifts: Phenomenological insights from
four contexts. *Journal of Consumer Research*, Vol. 17 No. 3, pp. 322–32.

Mikkonen, I., Vicdan, H., and Markkula, A. (2014), What not to wear? Oppositional
ideology, fashion, and governmentality in wardrobe self-help. *Consumption Markets & Culture*, Vol. 17 No. 3, pp. 254–73.

Moisander, J., Markkula, A., and Eräranta, K. (2010), Construction of consumer choice in the market: Challenges for environmental policy. *International Journal of Consumer Studies*, Vol. 34 No. 1, pp. 73–9.

Moschis, G.P. (2007), Stress and consumer behavior. *Journal of the Academy of Marketing Science*, Vol. 35 No. 3, pp. 430–44.

Nässén, J., and Larsson, J. (2015), Would shorter working time reduce greenhouse gas emissions? An analysis of time use and consumption in Swedish households. *Environment and Planning C: Government and Policy*, Vol. 33 No. 4, pp. 726–45.

Naturvårdsverket. (2017), Textile waste, www.naturvardsverket.se/Miljoarbete-i-samhallet/Miljoarbete-i-Sverige/Uppdelat-efter-omrade/Avfall/Avfallsforebyggande-program/Textil/, accessed March 24, 2017.

OECD (2017), https://stats.oecd.org/Index.aspx?DataSetCode=SNA_TABLE5

O'Guinn, T.C., and Faber, R.J. (1989), Compulsive buying: A phenomenological exploration. *Journal of Consumer Research*, pp. 147–57.

O'Guinn, T.C., and Faber, R.J. (1991), Mass communication and consumer behavior. *Handbook of Consumer Behavior*, Vol. 349, p. 400.

Pavia, T.M., and Mason, M.J. (2004), The reflexive relationship between consumer behavior and adaptive coping. *Journal of Consumer Research*, Vol. 31 No. 2, pp. 441–54.

Pearlin, L.I. (1983), "Role strains and personal stress", in Kaplan, H.B. (ed.), *Psychosocial Stress: Trends in Theory and Research*, Academic Press, New York, pp. 3–30.

Pearlin, L.I. (1989), The sociological study of stress. *Journal of Health and Social Behavior*, Vol. 30 No. 3, pp. 241–56.

Preda, A. (1999), The turn to things. *The Sociological Quarterly*, Vol. 40 No. 2, pp. 347–66.

Rafferty, K. (2011), Class-based emotions and the allure of fashion consumption. *Journal of Consumer Culture*, Vol. 11 No. 2, pp. 239–60.

Ransome, P. (2005), *Work, Consumption and Culture: Affluence and Social Change in the Twenty-First Century*, Sage, London.

Rockström, J., Steffen, W., Noone, K., Persson, Å., Chapin, F.S., Lambin, E.F., . . . and Nykvist, B. (2009), A safe operating space for humanity. *Nature*, Vol. 461 No. 7263, pp. 472–5.

Röpke, I. (2009), Theories of practice – New inspiration for ecological economic studies. *Ecological Economics*, Vol. 68, pp. 2490–7.

Roux, D., and Korchia, M. (2006), Am I what I wear? An exploratory study of symbolic meanings associated with secondhand clothing. *Advances in Consumer Research*, Vol. 33 No. 1, pp. 29–35.

Sanne, C. (2002), Willing consumers – Or locked-in? Policies for a sustainable consumption. *Ecological Economics*, Vol. 42 No. 1, pp. 273–87.

Sapolsky, R.M. (2004), *Why Zebras Don't Get Ulcers: The Acclaimed Guide to Stress, Stress-Related Diseases, and Coping – Now Revised and Updated*, Macmillan, New York.

Schatzki, T.R. (2001), Practice mind-ed orders. *The Practice Turn in Contemporary Theory*, Vol. 11.

Schiermer, B. (2011), Quasi-objects, cult objects and fashion objects: On two kinds of fetishism on display in modern culture. *Theory, Culture & Society*, Vol. 28 No. 1, pp. 81–102.

Schor, J.B. (2005), Sustainable consumption and worktime reduction. *Journal of Industrial Ecology*, Vol. 9 No. 1–2, pp. 37–50.

Shammin, M.R., and Bullard, C.W. (2009), Impact of cap-and-trade policies for reducing greenhouse gas emissions on US households. *Ecological Economics*, Vol. 86 No. 8, pp. 2432–2438.

Sheehan, B. (2010), *The Economics of Abundance: Affluent Consumption and the Global Economy*, Edward Elgar Publishing, Cheltenham, UK.

Shove, E. (2010), Beyond the ABC: Climate change policy and theories of social change. *Environment and Planning A*, Vol. 42 No. 6, pp. 1273–85.

Shove, E., Pantzar, M., and Watson, M. (2012), *The Dynamics of Social Practice: Everyday Life and How It Changes*, Sage Publications, Los Angeles.

Simmel, G. (1904), Fashion. *International Quarterly*, Vol. 10, pp. 130–55.

Solér, C., Baeza, J., and Svärd, C. (2015), Construction of silence on issues of sustainability through branding in the fashion market. *Journal of Marketing Management*, Vol. 31 No. 1–2, pp. 219–46.

Spaargaren, G. (2011), Theories of practices: Agency, technology, and culture: Exploring the relevance of practice theories for the governance of sustainable consumption practices in the new world-order. *Global Environmental Change*, Vol. 21 No. 3, pp. 813–22.

Statista. (2016), How many connected devices do you currently use? www.statista.com/statistics/365016/number-connected-devices-per-person-norway/

Statistics Sweden (2017).

Steg, L. (2015), "Environmental psychology and sustainable consumption", in Reisch, L.A. and Thørgersen, J. (eds.), *Handbook of Research on Sustainable Consumption*, Edward Elgar Publishing, Cheltenham, UK, pp. 70–83.

Sterling, P., and Eyer, J. 1988. "Allostasis: A new paradigm to explain arousal pathology", in Fisher, S. and Reason, J. (eds.), *Handbook of Life Stress, Cognition and Health*, John Wiley & Sons, Chichester, pp. 78–85.

Stern, P.C. (2000), New environmental theories: Toward a coherent theory of environmentally significant behavior. *Journal of Social Issues*, Vol. 56 No. 3, pp. 407–24.

Sujan, M., Sujan, H., Bettman, J., and Verhallen, T. (1999), "Sources of consumers' stress and their coping strategies", in Dubois, B., Lowrey, T., and Shrum, L. (eds.), *European Advances in Consumer Research*, Vol. 4, Association for Consumer Research, Provo, UT, pp. 182–7.

Swedish Environmental Protection Agency (2017).

The World Bank (2017), Global Consumption Database, http://datatopics.worldbank.org/consumption/

Thoits, P.A. (1995), Stress, coping, and social support processes: Where are we? What next? *Journal of Health and Social Behavior*, Vol. 35, pp. 53–79.

Thompson, C.J., and Haytko, D.L. (1997), Speaking of fashion: Consumers' uses of fashion discourses and the appropriation of countervailing cultural meanings. *Journal of Consumer Research*, Vol. 24 No. 1, pp. 15–42.

Trading Economics (2017), https://tradingeconomics.com/united-states/consumer-spending

Tukker, A., Cohen, M.J., Hubacek, K., and Mont, O. (2010), The impacts of household consumption and options for change. *Journal of Industrial Ecology*, Vol. 14 No. 1, pp. 13–30.

United Nations ComTrade (2016), https://comtrade.un.org/db/mr/rfCommodities List.aspx

US Bureau of Labor Statistics (2016), https://www.bls.gov/cex/

US Department of Energy (2017), https://energy.gov/eere/vehicles/fact-841-october-6-2014-vehicles-thousand-people-us-vs-other-world-regions

Wackernagel, M., Onisto, L., Bello, P., Linares, A.C., Falfán, I.S.L., Garcıa, J.M., . . . and Guerrero, M.G.S. (1999), National natural capital accounting with the ecological footprint concept. *Ecological Economics*, Vol. 29 No. 3, pp. 375–90.

Wackernagel, M., Schulz, N.B., Deumling, D., Linares, A.C., Jenkins, M., Kapos, V., . . . and Randers, J. (2002), Tracking the ecological overshoot of the human economy. *Proceedings of the National Academy of Sciences*, Vol. 99 No. 14, pp. 9266–71.

Währborg, P. (2002), *Stress och den nya ohälsan*, Natur och kultur, Stockholm.

Weiner, H. (1990), "Behavioral biology of stress and psychosomatic medicine", in Brown, M.R., Koob, G.F., and Rivier, C. (eds.), *Stress: Neurobiology and Neuroendocrinology*, Dekker, New York, pp. 23–51.

Wilk, R. (2002), Consumption, human needs, and global environmental change. *Global Environmental Change*, Vol. 12 No. 1, pp. 5–13.

Wilk, R. (2011), Consumption in an age of globalization and localization. *Beyond the Consumption Bubble*, pp. 37–51.

Woodruffe-Burton, H., and Elliott, R. (2005), Compensatory consumption and narrative identity theory. *Advances in Consumer Research*, Vol. 32 No. 1, pp. 461–5.

WRAP (2016), http://www.wrap.org.uk/sustainable-textiles

Yakhlef, A. (2015), Customer experience within retail environments: An embodied, spatial approach. *Marketing Theory*, Vol. 15 No. 4, pp. 545–64.

Young, W., and Middlemiss, L. (2012), A rethink of how policy and social science approach changing individuals' actions on greenhouse gas emissions. *Energy Policy*, Vol. 41, pp. 742–7.

2 The sustainability of affluent consumption from a stress perspective

The stress-theory framework presented in this book situates the affluent consumer body (which includes the mind) in the marketplace. Stress results from a situation that individuals perceive "as taxing or exceeding his or her resources and endangering his or her wellbeing" (Lazarus and Folkman, 1984, p. 19), and stress in the consumption context is defined as marketplace-induced strain resulting from environmental, social/internal or structural stressors that require the consumer to adjust his or her behaviour or cognition to maintain emotional and psychological control (Lazarus and Folkman, 1984; Moschis, 2007; Sapolsky, 2004; Thoits, 1995). An embodied stress perspective thus fully recognizes that macro-level marketplace structures and cultures (shaped to various extents by government policies) have an impact on micro-level consumption through our bodies (including our minds). In opposition to predominant streams of research within the field of sustainable consumption, where the body to a large degree is missing, the stress framework enables a merger of micro- and macro-level understandings of sustainable consumption.

Macro-level understandings of sustainable consumption

Macro-level perspectives on sustainable consumption include acknowledgement of dominant marketing practices (product representations in advertisement and branding as well as low prices/large quantities offerings) and subsequent consumer cultures, which include links between the material-intensity of consumption and working hours (Cohen, 2007; Cohen et al., 2010; Moisander et al., 2010; Schor, 1998, 2005; Röpke and Godesken, 2007; Varey, 2010). The body is largely missing in these studies, with the exception of bodily time spent working and discussions of how consumption activities compete for bodily time. Practice theory-oriented studies on sustainable consumption are categorized in this book as macro-level understandings of sustainable consumption, as "the practice turn" emphasizes the practical, collective and routine character of consumption (Halkier, 2013) even though its proponents would argue that there exists no level beyond that of social practice (see Shove and Walker, 2010). Theories of practice downplay individual agency and offer explanations of (un)sustainable consumption based on socio-material systems of infrastructures, innovation, routines and understandings (Welch and Warde, 2015). Sustainable consumption research informed by theories of practice can be divided into two converging streams of research (Welch and Warde, 2015): everyday practices enabled by configurations of material, meaning and competence (Shove, 2010; Shove et al., 2012) and cultural/political dimensions of consumption as the agency of citizen–consumers in global environmental governance and, more recently, collective normative frameworks (Dubuisson-Quellier and Gojard, 2016; Halkier, 2013; Spaargaren, 2011, 2013). Socio-technical regimes and experiments are yet another strand of macro-level practice theory-oriented sustainable consumption research that focus on the enablement of, and transitions to, sustainable modes of consumption through innovation and technological systems (Chappells and Medd, 2008; Cohen et al., 2010; Brown et al., 2003; Geels and Schot, 2007; Smith, 2007). Recent practice theorizing on sustainable consumption recognizes that "a combined focus on the technological and cultural dimensions of innovation in consumption practices is required" (Spaargaren, 2013, p. 246). Practice theory-oriented studies on sustainable consumption recognize the significant role of material elements for the production of sustainable social practices (Preda, 1999; Schatzki, 2001; Spaargaren, 2011; Shove, 2010). A social practice theory approach to sustainable consumption thus pays attention to material and bodily agency in terms of configuring consumer doings and consumption meanings (Röpke, 2009; Shove et al., 2012; Spaargaren, 2011). However, practice-oriented accounts of sustainable consumption discuss the body mainly in terms of bodily time spent performing various competing social practices, not as an organism acting within an experienced life-world (Röpke, 2009; Wilhite, 2012).

Micro-level understandings of sustainable consumption

Current micro-level understandings of sustainable consumption are dominated by cognitive/narrative-based individualistic approaches where material elements, the body in particular, are missing (Shove et al., 2012; Yakhlef, 2015). Cognitive-based environmental psychology studies deal with individual adoption of sustainable consumption patterns. A large body of research has focused on attitudes and values to explain pro-environmental consumer behaviour (Stern, 2000; Bamberg and Möser, 2007; Tanner and Kast, 2003). Unfortunately, attitudes and values have varying effects on actual pro-environmental consumer behaviour, and this well-known phenomenon has been labelled the attitude-behaviour gap (Young and Middlemiss, 2012; Vermeir and Verbeke, 2006; Gupta and Ogden, 2009), the knowledge-to-action gap (Markkula and Moisander, 2012) or the value-action gap (Shove, 2010; Steg, 2015). For example, only consumers whose pro-environmental values are activated and supported are likely to engage in sustainable consumption (Steg and Vlek, 2009; Steg, 2015).

The cultural perspective on sustainable consumption is primarily concerned with consumers' perceptions of sustainable consumption as part of identity-making (Autio et al., 2009; Cherrier et al., 2012) and how they identify with environmental issues in everyday practices (Connolly and Prothero, 2008). This equally cognitive/narrative-based stream of research departs from consumer discourse and ideology, framing consumers' interpretation and balancing autonomy and social affiliation through consumption (Autio et al., 2009; Belk et al., 2003; Connolly and Prothero, 2008; Markkula and Moisander, 2012; Mikkonen et al., 2014; Roux and Korchia, 2006; Thompson and Haytko, 1997). Literature on anti-consumption as rejection, reduction and reuse in opposition to cultures of consumption and as part of consumer identity-making (Chatzidakis and Lee, 2013; Cherrier, 2009) contributes to this body of research.

Both consumer culture and psychological studies approach sustainable consumption from a predominantly mind-focused perspective which excludes the body as the site for thoughts and emotions. Here, motivations to consume consist of emotions, beliefs, values, meanings, imagination and longing – which are cognitive and narrative-based constructs that represent explicit or implicit categories of cultural meaning. Sustainable consumption practices – which typically involve reduced or alternative consumption – are generally acknowledged as a means of constructing self-identity or enacting pro-environmental values within the dominant cultural codification system (Abrahamse and Steg, 2013; Autio et al., 2009; Connolly and Prothero, 2008; Dolan, 2002; Prothero et al., 2010; Prothero and Fitchett, 2000; Steg, 2015).

A stress framework: an embodied understanding of (un)sustainable affluent consumption

An embodied approach entails the recognition that consumers' thought content and emotions reside in the body. In opposition to predominant streams of research within the field of sustainable consumption where the body to a large degree is missing, the stress framework enables a merger of micro- and macro-level perspectives on sustainable consumption by understanding consumption as the outcome of the consumer body lived experience of the marketplace. An embodied perspective on sustainable consumption fully acknowledges the consumer body and adds to current scientific understandings of such consumption by recognizing the performative effect on consumer bodies of marketing practice.

Embodied consumer perception

In line with phenomenological thought, consumer experience of consumption objects is not solely produced by meanings and feelings, but is the outcome of the connection between the body and its life-world (Merleau-Ponty, 1962). Thus, embodied perception depends on previous experience inasmuch as previous experience conditions perception (Merleau-Ponty, 1962). This relational view on perception presupposes a dialectic between consumers' experiences of products and services and how these are experienced by shoppers (Yakhlef, 2015). From an embodied perspective, consumption activities are part of consumers' bodily experience of learned (culture-specific) sensory capacities (Gallagher, 2005; Yakhlef, 2015), not only as products of thinking and doing but as bodily sensory experiences of seeing, hearing, touching and feeling. Consumers' sensory capacities are thus acquired by being in the world, in this case, in the marketplace (Dreyfus, 2002; Gallagher, 2005; Yakhlef, 2015). In the consumption context, consumers' sensory experiences are provided or afforded by marketplaces (Gibson, 1979). The concept of affordances (Gibson, 1979) is instrumental in its capacity to situate consumer experience in the consumer life-world. The concept of affordances implies that agents (consumers) do not merely receive input passively and then process it. Rather, consumers are disposed to respond to the solicitations of things (offerings in the marketplace). Thus, consumers see market offerings from a specific perspective which "affords" certain action, i.e. ways of consumption. Consumer affordances vis-à-vis specific market offerings depend on past experience with such offerings (Dreyfus, 2002).

The concept of affordances, i.e. that consumers are predisposed (by the market) to act in specific ways, can be understood in terms of the idea of the intentional arc (Merleau-Ponty, 1962). The intentional arc implies that consumers' past experience of the marketplace becomes embodied, e.g. sedimented in the body including the mind, and creates pre-reflective bodily perceptive skills to understand this marketplace. Phenomenologically, taking the relational view between agent (consumer) and environment (marketplace) even further (Yakhlef, 2015), Merleau-Ponty's maximal grip (1962) illustrates the body (including the mind) as being solicited by and adjusting to situations by aiming for a body-environment equilibrium (Dreyfus, 2002). Hence, from an embodied perspective, narrative-based cognitive understandings and related feelings of the marketplace do not fully capture the mechanisms that produce and sustain consumption. Following Merleau-Ponty's *Phenomenology of Perception* (1962), consumption is not motivated by certain mental constructs, i.e. consumption is not goal directed, but should rather be viewed as an adjustment to a life-world (in this case, the relation between the affluent consumer and the affluent marketplace). The agent, in this case the consumer, perceives the socio-material marketplace through the body and adjusts its capacity to gain equilibrium in terms of having the situation under control, i.e. maximal grip (Dreyfus, 2002; Yakhlef, 2015).

The allostatic stress concept and the body as the locus of perceptual capacities

Allostatic balance (Sterling and Eyer, 1988) is a central stress concept – opposed to the earlier concept of homeostatic balance developed by psychologist Hans Selye (1956) – that emphasizes the central function of the brain in coordinating bodily reactions to stress. Internal or external strains (stressors) that give rise to potentially unhealthy functional changes in the body, as when situations are perceived by individuals as "taxing or exceeding his or her resources and endangering his or her wellbeing" (Lazarus and Folkman, 1984, p. 19), result in bodily efforts to restore bodily balance and control (Chrousos and Gold, 1992; Holmes and Rahe, 1967; Thoits, 1995; Sapolsky, 2004; Währborg, 2002; Weiner, 1991). The allostatic view of stress acknowledges the body as the locus of perceptual capacities through which we relate to, enact and experience stressors in the context of shopping (Merleau-Ponty, 1962). An allostatic perspective also implies that we can react to stressors in anticipation of what might be perceived as a strain (Sapolsky, 2004). The allostatic stress concept implies that an internal or external influence that is of a sufficient magnitude to result in functional changes of body balance – i.e. "the state in which all sorts of physiological measures are being kept at the optimal level" – will result in bodily efforts orchestrated by the brain (physiological, psychological and behavioural) to restore well-being (Sapolsky, 2004).

The allostatic stress concept captures the essence of Merleau-Ponty's idea of phenomenological perception in terms of the body's capacity to gain optimum, for example when maximizing visibility when adjusting the distance between body and objects in the environment to gain better focus, i.e. maximal grip of the situation (Dreyfus, 2002; Yakhlef, 2015). The body responds to threats to bodily balance (which includes cognitive understandings) with the aim of finding balance – what phenomenologists call optimum or equilibrium;

Acting is experienced as a steady flow of skilful activity in response to one's sense of the situation. Part of that experience is the sense that when one's situation deviates from some optimal body environment relationship, one's activity takes one closer to that optimum and thereby relieves the "tension" of the deviation. One does not need to know, nor can one normally express, what that optimum is. One's body is simply solicited by the situation to get into equilibrium with it (Dreyfus, 2002, p. 378).

Physical reactions to stressors include the rapid mobilization of energy from fat cells and muscles as well as increasing heart, breathing and blood pressure rates to transport energy quickly. As a consequence, growth and tissue repair is curtailed, and digestion and immunity are inhibited (Währborg, 2002). Psychological reactions to stressors include improved cognition and sensory skills, which are adaptive and helpful when facing potentially dangerous conditions (Währborg, 2002). Behavioural reactions to stressors are typically categorized as fight or flight, as humans tend to behave with hostility or to show signs of resignation when faced with stressors (Cannon, 1932; Sapolsky, 2004; Währborg, 2002). In sociological stress theory as applied in consumption studies, reactions to stress are conceptualized as coping, for instance efforts to restore balance following a stressor-induced disequilibrium (Lazarus and Folkman, 1984; Moschis, 2007; Pearlin, 1983). The coordinating function of the brain in allostatic thinking implies that stressors in the shopping context are assessed by the brain, which reacts to restore bodily balance when faced with strains that threaten balance in the body (including the mind). Hence, coping is what people do to attempt to lessen the effect of stressors experienced either as threat-related emotions that signal danger to personal well-being or as harm-related emotions such as anger (Lazarus and Folkman, 1984; Pearlin, 1989; Thoits, 1995).

Implications of an embodied approach on the understanding for affluent sustainable consumption as stress

The concept of affordances places understanding and feelings related to affluent consumption of products and services within, not outside of, the action possibilities provided by affluent marketplaces (Yakhlef, 2015). For example, "think ideal, feel bad" sequences related to the consumption of fashion objects that are assumed in studies on materialistic behaviours (Arndt et al., 2004; Burroughs et al., 2013), in material culture studies (Clarke and Miller, 2002) and in consumer research (Dittmar, 2008; Mick and DeMoss, 1990; Woodruffe-Burton and Elliott, 2005) are, according to an embodied view on consumption, provided – or afforded, to use Gibson's terminology – by the fashion marketplace. In addition, the embodied stress perspective on affluent consumption assumes that consumption object meanings and feelings such as those associated with "think ideal, feel bad "sequences are always accompanied by bodily sensory experiences. However, as already noted, the body is absent from studies addressing such sequences related to affluent consumption (e.g. Arndt et al., 2004; Burroughs et al., 2013; Clarke and Miller, 2002; Dittmar, 2008; Mick and DeMoss, 1990; Woodruffe-Burton and Elliott, 2005). The missing connection between body and mind in consumption studies, which is relevant for our understanding of sustainable affluent consumption, is restored by reading this literature through a sociological stress theory lens. A sociological stress theory framework acknowledges the impact of affluent marketplaces on the consumer body (as opposed to the impact on shoppers' minds and feelings, as described in the literature), which reacts when the bodily balance is threatened.

There are two main implications of viewing affluent consumption from a stress perspective. First, the non-cognitive "motor intentionality" referred to earlier as the "intentional arc" and "maximal grip", in terms of sedimented bodily learned perceptual skills (Merleau-Ponty, 1962; Yakhlef, 2015), recognizes pre-reflective bodily action in the marketplace. Research on consumption as bodily reactions and implicit body skills is currently lacking. A stress approach provides insights that can be instrumental in understanding current unsustainable patterns of affluent consumption as constant consumption of new variations of products already at our disposal and promoting more sustainable ways of consumption. Secondly, based on the reactive and constant adjusting capacity of the body when faced with disequilibrium due to variations in situational demand (Dreyfus, 2002; Merleau-Ponty, 1962), conceptualized as stress coping (Lazarus and Folkman, 1984; Pearlin, 1989; Thoits, 1995), it follows that affluent consumption is (in part) solicited by the marketplace. Thus, from a stress perspective, the scientific gaze should purposefully be directed to the relationship between the bodily demands of the affluent marketplace and subsequent affluent consumption. In Chapter 3, the sociological stress theory framework that forms the basis for this book is outlined.

Bibliography

Abrahamse, W., and Steg, L. (2013), Social influence approaches to encourage resource conservation: A meta-analysis. *Global Environmental Change*, Vol. 23 No. 6, pp. 1773–85.

Arndt, J.S., Solomon, K.T., and Sheldon, K.M. (2004), The urge to splurge: A terror management account of materialism and consumer behavior. *Journal of Consumer Psychology*, Vol. 14 No. 3, pp. 198–212.

Autio, M., Heiskanen, E., and Heinonen, V. (2009), Narratives of 'green' consumers – The antihero, the environmental hero and the anarchist. *Journal of Consumer Behaviour*, Vol. 8 No. 1, pp. 40–53.

Bamberg, S., and Möser, G. (2007), Twenty years after Hines, Hungerford, and Tomera: A new meta-analysis of psycho-social determinants of pro-environmental behaviour. *Journal of Environmental Psychology*, Vol. 27 No. 1, pp. 14–25.

Belk, R., Ger, G., and Askegaard, S. (2003), The fire of desire: A multisited inquiry into consumer passion. *Journal of Consumer Research*, Vol. 30 No. 3, pp. 326–51.

Boström, M., and Klintman, M. (2009), The green political food consumer: A critical analysis of the research and policies. *Anthropology of Food*, Vol. S5.

Brown, H.S., Vergragt, P., Green, K., and Berchicci, L. (2003), Learning for sustainability transition through bounded socio-technical experiments in personal mobility. *Technology Analysis & Strategic Management*, Vol. 15 No. 3, pp. 291–315.

Burroughs, J.E., Chaplin, L.N., Pandelaere, M., Norton, M.I., Ordabayeva, N., Gunz, A., and Dinauer, L. (2013), Using motivation theory to develop a transformative consumer research agenda for reducing materialism in society. *Journal of Public Policy & Marketing*, Vol. 32 No. 1, pp. 18–31.

Cannon, W.B. (1932), *The Wisdom of the Body*, Norton, New York.

Chappells, H., and Medd, W. (2008), What is fair? Tensions between sustainable and equitable domestic water consumption in England and Wales. *Local Environment*, Vol. 13 No. 8, pp. 725–41.

Chatzidakis, A., and Lee, M.S. (2013), Anti-consumption as the study of reasons against. *Journal of Macromarketing*, Vol. 33 No. 3, pp. 190–203.

Cherrier, H., Szuba, M., and Özcaglar-Toulouse, N. (2012), Barriers to downward carbon emission: Exploring sustainable consumption in face of the glass floor. *Journal of Marketing Management*, Vol. 28 No. 3–4, pp. 397–419.

Chrousos, G.P., and Gold, P.W. (1992), The concepts of stress and stress system disorders: Overview of physical and behavioral homeostasis. *Journal of the American Medical Association*, Vol. 267 No. 9, pp. 1244–52.

Clarke, A., and Miller, D. (2002), Fashion and anxiety. *Fashion Theory*, Vol. 6 No. 2, pp. 191–214.

Cohen, M.J. (2007), Consumer credit, household financial management, and sustainable consumption. *International Journal of Consumer Studies*, Vol. 31 No. 1, pp. 57–65.

Cohen, M.J., Brown, H.S., and Vergragt, P.J. (2010), Individual consumption and systemic societal transformation: Introduction to the special issue. *Sustainability: Science, Practice, & Policy*, Vol. 6 No. 2.

Connolly, J., and Prothero, A. (2008), Green consumption: Life-politics, risk and contradictions. *Journal of Consumer Culture*, Vol. 8 No. 1, pp. 117–45.

Dittmar, H. (2008), *Consumer Culture, Identity and Well-Being*, Psychology Press, New York.

Dolan, P. (2002), The sustainability of 'sustainable consumption'. *Journal of Macromarketing*, Vol. 22 No. 2, pp. 170–81.

Dreyfus, H.L. (2002), Intelligence without representation: The relevance of phenomenology to scientific explanation. *Phenomenology and the Cognitive Sciences*, Vol. 1 No. 4, pp. 367–83.

Dubuisson-Quellier, S., and Gojard, S. (2016), Why are food practices not (more) environmentally friendly in France? The role of collective standards and symbolic boundaries in food practices. *Environmental Policy and Governance*, Vol. 26 No. 2, pp. 89–100.

Gallagher, S. (2005), *How the Body Shapes the Mind*, Oxford University Press, New York.

Geels, F.W., and Schot, J. (2007), Typology of sociotechnical transition pathways. *Research Policy*, Vol. 36 No. 3, pp. 399–417.

Gibson, J.J. (1979), "The theory of affordances", in *The Ecological Approach to Visual Perception*, Houghton Mifflin Harcourt, Hopewell, pp. 56–60.

Gram-Hanssen, K., and Bech-Danielsen, K. (2004), House, home and identity from a consumption perspective. *Housing, Theory and Society*, Vol. 21 No. 1, pp. 17–26.

Gupta, S., and Ogden, D.T. (2009), To buy or not to buy? A social dilemma perspective on green buying. *Journal of Consumer Marketing*, Vol. 26 No. 6, pp. 376–91, www.emeraldinsight.com/10.1108/07363760910988201, accessed February 6, 2014.

Halkier, B. (2013), "Sustainable lifestyles in a new economy: A practice theoretical perspective on change behavior campaigns and sustainability issues", in Cohen, M.J., Brown, H.S., and Vergragt, P.J. (eds.), *Innovations in Sustainable Consumption: New Economics, Socio-Technical Transitions and Social Practices*, Edward Elgar Publishing, Cheltenham, UK, pp. 209–28.

Holmes, T.H., and Rahe, R.H. (1967), The social readjustment rating scale. *Journal of Psychosomatic Research*, Vol. 11 No. 2, pp. 213–8.

Lazarus, R.S., and Folkman, S. (1984), *Stress, Appraisal, and Coping*, Springer Publishing Company, New York.

Lehner, M., Mont, O., and Heiskanen, E. (2016), Nudging – A promising tool for sustainable consumption behaviour? *Journal of Cleaner Production*, Vol. 134, pp. 166–77.

Markkula, A., and Moisander, J. (2012), Discursive confusion over sustainable consumption: A discursive perspective on the perplexity of marketplace knowledge. *Journal of Consumer Policy*, Vol. 35 No. 1, pp. 105–25.

Merleau-Ponty, M. (1962), *Phenomenology of Perception*, Routledge, London.

Mick, D.G., and Demoss, M. (1990), Self-gifts: Phenomenological insights from four contexts. *Journal of Consumer Research*, Vol. 17 No. 3, pp. 322–32.

Mikkonen, I., Vicdan, H., and Markulla, A. (2014), What not to wear? Oppositional ideology, fashion, and governmentality in wardrobe self-help. *Consumption, Markets & Culture*, Vol. 17 No. 3, pp. 254–73.

Moisander, J., Markkula, A., and Eräranta, K. (2010), Construction of consumer choice in the market: Challenges for environmental policy. *International Journal of Consumer Studies*, Vol. 34 No. 1, pp. 73–9.

Moschis, G.P. (2007), Stress and consumer behavior. *Journal of the Academy of Marketing Science*, Vol. 35 No. 3, pp. 430–44.

Pearlin, L. (1983), "Role strains and personal stress", in Kaplan, H.B. (ed.), *Psychosocial Stress: Trends in Theory and Research*, Academic Press, New York, pp. 3–30.

Pearlin, L. (1989), The sociological study of stress. *Journal of Health and Social Behavior*, Vol. 30 No. 3, pp. 241–56.

Preda, A. (1999), The turn to things. *The Sociological Quarterly*, Vol. 40 No. 2, pp. 347–66.

Prothero, A., Dobscha, S., Freund, J., Kilbourne, W.E., Luchs, M.E., Ozanne, L.K., and Thøgersen, J. (2010), Sustainable consumption: Opportunities for consumer research and public policy. *Journal of Public Policy & Marketing*, Vol. 30 No. 1, pp. 31–8.

Prothero, A., and Fitchett, J.A. (2000), Greening capitalism: Opportunities for a green commodity. *Journal of Macromarketing*, Vol. 20 No. 1, pp. 46–55.

Röpke, I. (2009), Theories of practice – New inspiration for ecological economic studies. *Ecological Economics*, Vol. 68, pp. 2490–7.

Ropke, I., and Godskesen, M. (2007), Leisure activities, time and environment. *International Journal of Innovation and Sustainable Development*, Vol. 2 No. 2, pp. 155–174.

Roux, D., and Korchia, M. (2006), Am I what I wear? An exploratory study of symbolic meanings associated with second hand clothing. *Advances in Consumer Research*, Vol. 33, pp. 29–35.

Sapolsky, R.M. (2004), *Why Zebras Don't Get Ulcers: The Acclaimed Guide to Stress, Stress-Related Diseases, and Coping – Now Revised and Updated*, Macmillan, New York.

Schatzki, T.R. (2001), Practice mind-ed orders. *The Practice Turn in Contemporary Theory*, Vol. 11.

Schor, J.B. (1998), *The Overspent American, Upscaling, Downshifting, and the New Consumer*, Basic Books, New York.

Schor, J.B. (2005), Prices and quantities: Unsustainable consumption and the global economy. *Ecological Economics*, Vol. 55 No. 3, pp. 309–20.

Selye, H. (1956), *The Stress of Life*, McGraw-Hill, New York.

Shove, E. (2010), Beyond the ABC: Climate change policy and theories of social change. *Environment and Planning A*, Vol. 42 No. 6, pp. 1273–85.

Shove, E., Pantzar, M., and Watson, M. (2012), *The Dynamics of Social Practice: Everyday Life and How It Changes*, Sage Publications, Los Angeles.

Shove, E., and Walker, G. (2010), Governing transitions in the sustainability of everyday life. *Research Policy*, Vol. 39 No. 4, pp. 471–6.

Smith, A. (2007), Translating sustainabilities between green niches and socio-technical regimes. *Technology Analysis & Strategic Management*, Vol. 19 No. 4, pp. 427–50.

Spaargaren, G. (2011), Theories of practices: Agency, technology, and culture: Exploring the relevance of practice theories for the governance of sustainable consumption practices in the new world-order. *Global Environmental Change*, Vol. 21 No. 3, pp. 813–22.

Spaargaren, G. (2013), "The cultural dimension of sustainable consumption practices: An exploration in theory and policy", in Cohen, M.J., Brown, H.S., and Vergragt, P.J. (eds.), *Innovations in Sustainable Consumption: New Economics, Socio-technical Transitions and Social Practices*, Edward Elgar Publishing, Cheltenham, UK, pp. 229–51.

Steg, L. (2015), "Environmental psychology and sustainable consumption", in Reisch, L.A. and Thørgersen, J. (eds.), *Handbook of Research on Sustainable Consumption*, Edward Elgar Publishing, Cheltenham, UK, pp. 70–83.

Steg, L., and Vlek, C. (2009), Encouraging pro-environmental behaviour: An integrative review and research agenda. *Journal of Environmental Psychology*, Vol. 29 No. 3, pp. 309–17.

Sterling, P., and Eyer, J. (1988), "Allostasis: A new paradigm to explain arousal pathology", in Fisher, S. and Reason, J. (eds.), *Handbook of Life Stress, Cognition and Health*, John Wiley & Sons, Chichester, pp. 78–85.

Stern, P.C. (2000), New environmental theories: Toward a coherent theory of environmentally significant behavior. *Journal of Social Issues*, Vol. 56 No. 3, pp. 407–24.

Tanner, C., and Wölfing Kast, S. (2003), Promoting sustainable consumption: Determinants of green purchases by Swiss consumers. *Psychology & Marketing*, Vol. 20 No. 10, pp. 883–902.

Thoits, P.A. (1995), Stress, coping, and social support processes: Where are we? What next? *Journal of Health and Social Behavior*, Vol. 35, pp. 53–79.

Thompson, C.T., and Haytko, D.L. (1997), Speaking of fashion: Consumers' uses of fashion discourses and the appropriation of countervailing cultural meanings. *Journal of Consumer Research*, Vol. 24 No. 1, pp. 15–42.

Varey, R.J. (2010), Marketing means and ends for a sustainable society: A welfare agenda for transformative change. *Journal of Macromarketing*, Vol. 30 No. 2, pp. 112–26.

Vermeir, I., and Verbeke, W. (2006), Sustainable food consumption: Exploring the consumer 'attitude – Behavioral intention' gap. *Journal of Agricultural and Environmental Ethics*, Vol. 19 No. 2, pp. 169–94, http://link.springer.com/10.1007/s10806-005-5485-3, accessed January 23, 2014.

Wåhrborg, P. (2002), *Stress och den nya ohälsan*, Natur och kultur, Stockholm.

Weiner, H. (1991), "Behavioral biology of stress and psychosomatic medicine", in Brown, M.R., Koob, G.F., and Rivier, C. (eds.), *Stress: Neurobiology and Neuroendocrinology*, CRC Press, New York, pp 23–54.

Welch, D., and Warde, A. (2015), "Theories of practice and sustainable consumption", in Reisch, L.A. and Thørgersen, J. (eds.), *Handbook of Research on Sustainable Consumption*, Edward Elgar Publishing, Cheltenham, UK, pp. 84–100.

Wilhite, H. (2012), Towards a better accounting of the roles of body, things and habits in consumption. *Collegium*, Vol. 12, pp. 87–99.

Woodruffe-Burton, H., and Elliott, R. (2005), Compensatory consumption and narrative identity theory. *Advances in Consumer Research*, Vol. 32 No. 1, pp. 461–5.

Yakhlef, A. (2015), Customer experience within retail environments: An embodied, spatial approach. *Marketing Theory*.

Young, W., and Middlemiss, L. (2012), A rethink of how policy and social science approach changing individuals' actions on greenhouse gas emissions. *Energy Policy*, Vol. 41, pp. 742–7.

3 A sociological stress theory framework

In this chapter, the embodied perspective on affluent consumption is related to sociological stress theory. To discuss consumption from a stress perspective, I employ a sociological stress theory framework that encompasses the relationship between stressors, bodily reactions and stress coping strategies (Duhachek, 2005; Holahan and Moos, 1987; Holmes and Rahe, 1967; Pearlin, 1989; Sapolsky, 2004; Thoits, 1995; Weiner, 1990). The stress framework (Figure 3.1), as described from a sociological perspective, can be illustrated with a S-O-R model. In this model, internal/external and structural stressors produce reactions in the body (including the mind), which responds by restoring bodily balance and functions through coping (Duhachek, 2005; Holahan and Moos, 1987; Holmes and Rahe, 1967; Pearlin, 1989; Sapolsky, 2004; Thoits, 1995; Weiner, 1990).

Marketplace-induced stressors as affluent consumer role strains

Stressors are internal or external influences that are of a sufficient magnitude to result in functional changes in body balance and subsequent loss of control (Sapolsky, 2004). In Chapter 1, we defined stress in the consumption context as marketplace-induced environmental, social/internal or structural stressors that require the consumer to adjust his or her behaviour or cognition to maintain emotional and psychological control (Lazarus and Folkman, 1984; Moschis, 2007; Sapolsky, 2004; Thoits, 1995). Marketplace-induced stressors refer to aspects of consumers' marketplace experience that are perceived "as taxing or exceeding his or her resources and endangering his or her wellbeing" (Lazarus and Folkman, 1984, p. 19). External, or environmental, affluent marketplace-induced stressors are connected to the information- and stimuli-rich affluent marketplace (Eppler and Mengis, 2004; Jacoby, 1984; Luce, 1998; Malhotra, 1984; Moschis, 2007). From an allostatic stress perspective, consumers can react to marketplace stressors in anticipation of what might be perceived as a strain (Sapolsky,

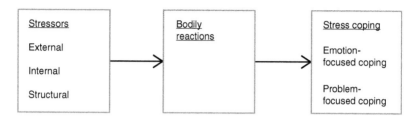

Figure 3.1 A sociological stress model

2004). Internal and social affluent marketplace-induced stressors are connected to anticipated stress (as the theory on allostatic stress recognizes that we can learn to perceive potential future stress based on experience). Examples of internalized stressors are, by social norms, to constantly partake in consumption activities and adhere to consumer culture ideals. For example, the continuous redefinition of socially desirable fashion objects in Western affluent consumer cultures explains why choice of clothes can be associated with considerable stress and anxiety (Dittmar, 2008; Halliwell et al., 2007; Luce, 1998; Moschis, 2007). Structural marketplace induced stressors are related to life-style conditions that face Western affluent consumers. Examples of such structural stressors are time scarcity and existential strains (Glorieux et al, 2010; Reisch, 2001; Sullivan, 2008).

Two types of stressors, acute and chronic strains, are described in psychological and sociological stress research (Moschis, 2007; Pearlin, 1989; Thoits, 1995). Stress related to consumption is commonly understood as enduring and chronic, not acute, as such stress is interrelated with established market-practice and consumer role strains (Moschis, 2007; Pearlin, 1989). Role overload is one chronic consumer role strain proposed in the stress literature (Pearlin, 1989). Affluent consumer role overload implies that the demands of the affluent marketplace exceed affluent consumer capacity (Pearlin, 1989). Studies on consumer stress support the proposition that affluent consumers are overloaded by the many product choices and product representations available in the marketplace and that this role overload leads to stressful choice uncertainty (Luce, 1998; Moschis, 2007). Affluent consumer role overload is also associated with a large number of opportunities to use mediated experiences, i.e. consumers' ability to experience product offerings that are separated in space and time (Elliott, 2004). Consumer role overload has predominantly been dealt with from mind-based scientific perspectives. The bodily dimension of consumer role overload suggests that consumers' role overload "is in a constant operation to skillfully cope with new situational demands in an attempt to be attuned to the environment and to maintain grip on it" (Yakhlef, 2015, p. 14). Using the phenomenological terminology of the maximal grip, consumer role overload is always parallel to the bodily skilful activity of achieving an optimal grip on the situation (Dreyfus, 2002; Merleau-Ponty, 1962).

Stress mediators in a marketplace setting

The impact of marketplace stressors on individual affluent consumers depends to a large degree on consumer coping strategies and on stress mediators. The most important stress mediators in a consumption setting are stressors' potential threats to cultural/social values and consumers' ability to control and predict them (Moschis, 2007; Pearlin, 1989; Sapolsky, 2004). This means that marketplace-induced internalized stressors that are connected to highly valued social and cultural norms, as for example socially desirable fashion objects, are perceived as more stressful than less socially desirable consumption objects. In addition, it means that an environmental marketplace where unexpected visual designs, noise etc. are used to stimulate consumers and promote consumption is experienced as stressful to a greater extent than a marketplace environment without such unexpected sensory stimuli. According to the stress literature, the impact of stressors, in this case role strains, varies between consumers. In other words, role strains produce different demands on individual affluent consumer bodies depending on consumers' adherence to cultural/social values linked to specific marketplace stressors and consumers' ability to predict such stressors (and hence control them).

Bodily reactions to marketplace stressors

When stressed, our bodies react by adjusting physically, psychologically or through changes in behaviour. Stress causes the body to rapidly mobilize energy from fat cells and muscles and increase pulse, breathing and blood pressure in order to transport energy quickly (Chrousos and Gold, 1992; Währborg, 2002). An embodied stress perspective implies that perceived stressors are accompanied by bodily experiences of arousal (Dawson et al., 1990; Mehta et al., 2013; O'Guinn and Faber, 1989; van Rompay et al., 2012). Arousal is defined as "the neurophysiological basis underlying all processes in the human organism. Thus, arousal is the basis of emotions, motivation, information processing, and behavioral reactions" (Bagozzi et al., 1999; Groeppel-Klein, 2005, p. 428). Bodily arousal reflects "the degree to which a person feels excited, stimulated, alert, or active in the situation" (Donovan and Rossiter, 1982, p. 38). Arousal can vary from deep sleep to panic and is produced by a combination of internal reactions (e.g.

thought content and emotion) and external stimuli (Boucsein et al., 2001; Mehrabian and Russell, 1974). Stress literature describes primary and secondary cognitive appraisal of person – environment encounters (Folkman and Lazarus, 1985). Primary appraisal is linked to bodily arousal as an encounter can be experienced as irrelevant (having no significance for one's well-being), positive/benign or stressful. "Stressful appraisals are characterized by threat, challenge, or harm-loss. Threat refers to the potential for harm or loss; challenge refers to the potential for growth, mastery, or gain; and harm-loss refers to injury already done, as in harm to a friendship, health, or self-esteem" (Folkman and Lazarus, 1985, p. 152). As will be described more in detail in Part 2 of this book, the literature provides ample evidence that stimuli-rich marketplaces filled with colour, music, scent, lighting and symbols increase consumers' arousal levels. Heightened levels of arousal are perceived as non-pleasant regardless of whether they stem from positive or negative emotions (Bitner, 1992; Donovan and Rossiter, 1982; Garlin and Owen, 2006; Groeppel-Klein, 2005; Tuch et al., 2009; Mehrabian and Russell, 1974; van Rompay et al., 2012; Kaltcheva and Weitz, 2006). Further psychological literature suggests that stimuli- or information-rich marketplaces create feelings of overload and confusion (Chen et al., 2009; Lee and Lee, 2004). In addition, as will be explored in Chapter 5, the continuous need for experiential input in individual identity-making of consumer culture (Cherrier et al., 2012; Elliott, 2004; Jantzen et al., 2012; Mikkonen et al., 2014), which is provided in the affluent marketplace, increases consumers' arousal levels.

Behavioural reactions to stress are categorized as fight or flight. When stressed, humans tend either to behave with hostility or show signs of resignation (Cannon, 1932). Consumption stress research, however, indicates that consumers cope with stress primarily through fight rather than flight responses.

Coping with marketplace stressors (in the marketplace)

Sociological stress theory conceptualizes coping, i.e. an evaluation of the options and resources at hand to manage stressors, as secondary appraisal (primary appraisal is concerned with evaluating a situation as stressful or not). Coping aims to restore bodily balance and control following a stress-inducing disequilibrium (Lazarus and Folkman, 1984; Moschis, 2007; Pearlin, 1983). Thus stressors are assessed by the brain, which reacts to restore bodily balance when confronted by strains that threaten bodily (including mental) balance. Coping involves bodily adjustment, including both cognitive and pre-reflective adjustments. From an embodied perspective, coping is not understood as goal-directed, but rather as a "steady flow of skillful activity in response to one's sense of the situation" (Yakhlef, 2015).

Individuals' coping strategies vary. Literature on stress suggests different stress coping strategies. Stress-coping strategies are categorized as active (approach) coping through modifying the stressor (problem-focused strategies) and avoidance coping, which aims to reduce the tension caused by the stressor (emotion-focused strategies) (Holahan and Moos, 1987; Lazarus and Folkman, 1984; Sapolsky, 2004; Thoits, 1995). Previous research on consumers' stress coping addresses consumption as a means to cope with stress following life events (Lee et al., 2001), daily hassles (Celuch and Showers, 1991) or meanings and emotions related to technological products (Mick and Fournier, 1998). However, there is a general lack of research investigating consumers' stress coping in the context of chronic marketplace strains. In the consumption context, problem-focused coping implies that marketplace stressors are coped with through actions such as consciously changing consumer behaviour or seeking information about consumption alternatives (Duhachek, 2005; Moschis, 2007). Emotion-focused coping manages emotions towards stressors through different cognitive and behavioural processes (Duhachek, 2005; Moschis, 2007). Consumer stress research indicates that consumers combine problem-focused and emotion-focused coping (Luce, 1998; Mick and Fournier, 1998; Sujan et al., 1999) but that support-seeking coping as an emotion-focused coping strategy dominates in a Western consumer culture context. The construct of self-efficacy as the perception of one's own ability to cope with stress-related emotions is used to explain why consumers who believe they are capable of coping tend to seek social support instead of using avoidance or active coping strategies when faced with marketplace stressors that lead to threat emotions (Duhachek, 2005; Sujan et al., 1999). Duhachek's work on consumer coping (2005) is instrumental in understanding the reasons behind this book's argument that consumers in the affluent marketplace mainly deal with marketplace-induced stress through support-seeking coping. Duhachek hypothesizes that consumers experiencing the stress-related emotion of threat in conjunction with high self-efficacy are likely to engage in support-seeking stress coping, whereas those with low self-efficacy are likely to engage in other kinds of avoidance coping. Consumers experiencing the stress-related emotion of anger in conjunction with high self-efficacy are likely to engage in active coping strategies (problem-focused strategies). Folkman and Lazarus (1986) suggest that coping strategies depend on whether situations are appraised as changeable or unchangeable. They propose that emotion – focused coping is more frequent when stressors are perceived as unchangeable and problem-focused coping more frequent in encounters that are appraised as changeable. Given that outdated versions of products in fashion industries potentially are experienced as a threat to cultural/social values when new desirable product designs are launched, it is likely that the emotion of threat is the dominant stress-related emotion in a consumption context. The affluent marketplace consumption context, with plentiful access to financial resources to consume as well as support structures such as peer advice, suggests that support-seeking dominates affluent consumers' coping with marketplace-induced stress. Support-seeking coping is a likely coping strategy among affluent, self-efficient consumers, i.e. those who believe that adequate coping is within their reach (Sujan et al., 1999; Duhachek, 2005). As reliance on expert systems – such as advertising, brands, one's peers or aesthetic experts, which can provide guidelines as to what to consume – is widely available in the affluent marketplace (Clarke and Miller, 2002; Warde, 1994; Turnbull et al., 2000; Woodward, 2006), support-seeking coping is afforded by the marketplace (Dreyfus, 2002). The affluent marketplace enables coping (aiming to restore balance from consumption stress) in the form of consumption.

A stress model of sustained affluent consumption

The S-O-R model in Figure 3.1 does not fully recognize the embodied stress perspective of this book. The understanding of affluent consumer marketplace-induced stress as a chronic role strain primarily coped with by support-seeking strategies implies that (1) the affluent consumption marketplace provides stressors that (2) to a large extent are coped with through learned strategies that in many cases are provided by the marketplace (advertisement, expert advice etc.) and that (3) these coping strategies involve consumption. From an embodied perspective, the sociological stress model in Figure 3.1 is re-conceptualized to reflect the body as constantly responding to threats to bodily balance with the aim of finding balance, or what phenomenologists call optimum or equilibrium. The embodied stress model in Figure 3.2 posits marketplace-induced stressors within the marketplace in line with the idea of the intentional arc (Merleau-Ponty, 1962). According to the phenomenological concept of the intentional arc, consumers' experience of the marketplace becomes sedimented in the body, including the mind. Hence, experience of access to support-seeking coping resources creates pre-reflective bodily skills to cope by means of support-seeking.

Figure 3.2 forms the basis for my suggestion of how stress, caused by and in the affluent marketplace, maintains unsustainable levels of consumption. Merleau-Ponty's concept of the maximal grip (1962) illustrates how we can understand the consumer body (including the mind) as adjusting to the marketplace by seeking a body-environment equilibrium (Dreyfus, 2002). Using Gibson's concept of affordances (1979), we can see that affluent consumers are primed to respond to the solicitations of the affluent marketplace that afford specific bodily experiences (Dreyfus, 2002): in other

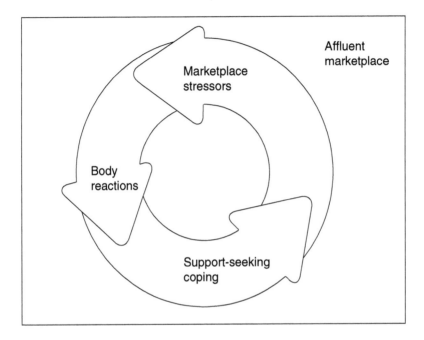

Figure 3.2 An embodied stress model

words, certain bodily reactions and coping strategies. The evidence base for this proposed model is theoretical. The embodied stress model is supported by data from various scientific fields – materialism studies, consumer culture studies, psychology, neuromarketing, information overload studies, sensory marketing etc. – that cover different facets of affluent consumption-related meanings and emotions. This data has been integrated with evidence from sociological and psychological stress research and will be described in detail in the next section of this book.

Bibliography

Bagozzi, R.P., Gopinath, M., and Nyer, P.U. (1999), The role of emotions in marketing. *Journal of the Academy of Marketing Science*, Vol. 27 No. 2, pp. 184–206.

Bitner, M.J. (1992), Servicescapes: The impact of physical surroundings on customers and employees. *Journal of Marketing*, Vol. 56 No. 2, pp. 57–71.

Boucsein, K., Weniger, G., Mursch, K., Steinhoff, B.J., and Irle, E. (2001), Amygdala lesion in temporal lobe epilepsy subjects impairs associative learning of emotional facial expressions. *Neuropsychologia*, Vol. 39 No. 3, pp. 231–6.

Cannon, W.B. (1932), *The Wisdom of the Body*, Norton, New York.

Carver, C.S., and Scheier, M.F. (1994), Situational coping and coping dispositions in a stressful transaction. *Journal of Personality and Social Psychology*, Vol. 66 No. 1, p. 184.

Celuch, K., and Showers, L. (1991), It's time to stress stress. The stress-purchase/ consumption relationship: Suggestions for research. *Advances in Consumer Research*, Vol. 18 No. 1, pp. 284–9.

Chen, Y.C., Shang, R.A., and Kao, C.Y. (2009), The effects of information overload on consumers' subjective state towards buying decision in the internet shopping environment. *Electronic Commerce Research and Applications*, Vol. 8 No. 1, pp. 48–58.

Chrousos, G.P., and Gold, P.W. (1992), The concepts of stress and stress system disorders: Overview of physical and behavioral homeostasis. *JAMA*, Vol. 267 No. 9, pp. 1244–52.

Clarke, A., and Miller, D. (2002), Fashion and anxiety. *Fashion Theory*, Vol. 6 No. 2, pp. 191–213.

Dawson, S., Bloch, P.H., and Ridgway, N. (1990), Shopping motives, emotional states, and retail outcomes. *Journal of Retailing*, Vol. 66 No. 4, p. 408.

Dittmar, H. (2008), *Consumer Culture, Identity and Well-Being*, Psychology Press, New York.

Donovan, R.J., and Rossiter, J.R. (1982), Store atmosphere: An environmental psychology approach. *Journal of Retailing*, Vol. 58 No. 1, pp. 34–57.

Dreyfus, H.L. (2002), Intelligence without representation – Merleau-Ponty's critique of mental representation the relevance of phenomenology to scientific explanation. *Phenomenology and the Cognitive Sciences*, Vol. 1 No. 4, pp. 367–83.

Duhachek, A. (2005), Coping: A multidimensional, hierarchical framework of responses to stressful consumption episodes. *Journal of Consumer Research*, Vol. 32 No. 1, pp. 41–53.

Elliott, R. (2004), "Making up people: Consumption as a symbolic vocabulary for the construction of identity", in Ekström, K.M., and Brembeck, H. (eds.), *Elusive Consumption*, Berg Publishers, Oxford, pp. 11–25.

Eppler, M.J., and Mengis, J. (2004), The concept of information overload: A review of literature from organization science, accounting, marketing, MIS, and related disciplines. *Information Society*, Vol. 20 No. 5, pp. 325–44.

Folkman, S., and Lazarus, R.S. (1985), If it changes it must be a process: study of emotion and coping during three stages of a college examination. *Journal of personality and social psychology*, Vol. 48 No. 1, p. 150.

Gibson, J.J. (1979), "The theory of affordances", in *The Ecological Approach to Visual Perception*, Houghton Mifflin Harcourt, Hopewell, pp. 56–60.

Glorieux, I., Laurijssen, I., Minnen, J., and van Tienoven, T.P. (2010), In search of the harried leisure class in contemporary society: time-use surveys and patterns of leisure time consumption. *Journal of Consumer policy*, Vol. 33 No. 2, pp. 163–181.

Groeppel-Klein, A. (2005), Arousal and consumer in-store behavior. *Brain Research Bulletin*, Vol. 67 No. 5, pp. 428–37.

Halliwell, E., Dittmar, H., and Orsborn, A. (2007), The effects of exposure to muscular male models among men: Exploring the moderating role of gym use and exercise motivation. *Body Image*, Vol. 4 No. 3, pp. 278–87.

Holahan, C.J., and Moos, R.H. (1987), Personal and contextual determinants of coping strategies. *Journal of Personality and Social Psychology*, Vol. 52 No. 5, pp. 946–55.

Holmes, T.H., and Rahe, R.H. (1967), The social readjustment rating scale. *Journal of Psychosomatic Research*, Vol. 11 No. 2, pp. 213–18.

Jacoby, J. (1984), Perspectives on information overload. *Journal of Consumer Research*, Vol. 10 No. 4, pp. 432–5.

Kaltcheva, V.D., and Weitz, B.A. (2006), When should a retailer create an exciting store environment? *Journal of Marketing*, Vol. 70 No. 1, pp. 107–18.

Lazarus, R.S., and Folkman, S. (1984), *Stress, Appraisal, and Coping*, Springer Publishing Company, New York.

Lee, B.-K., and Lee, W.-N. (2004), The effect of information overload on consumer choice quality in an on-line environment. *Psychology and Marketing*, Vol. 21 No. 3, pp. 159–83.

Lee, E., Moschis, G., and Mathur, A. (2001), A study on life events and changes in patronage preferences. *Journal of Business Research*, Vol. 54 No. 1, pp. 25–38.

Luce, M.F. (1998), Choosing to avoid: Coping with negatively emotion-laden consumer decisions. *Journal of Consumer Research*, Vol. 24 No. 4, pp. 409–33.

Malhotra, N.K. (1984), Reflections on the information overload paradigm in consumer decision making. *Journal of Consumer Research*, Vol. 10 No. 4, pp. 436–40.

Mehrabian, A., and Russell, J.A. (1974), *An Approach to Environmental Psychology*, MIT Press, Cambridge, MA.

Mehta, R., Sharma, N.K., and Swami, S. (2013), The impact of perceived crowding on consumers' store patronage intentions: Role of optimal stimulation level and shopping motivation. *Journal of Marketing Management*, Vol. 29 No. 7–8, pp. 812–35.

Merleau-Ponty, M. (1962), *Phenomenology of Perception*, Routledge, London.

Mick, D.G., and Fournier, S. (1998), Paradoxes of technology: Consumer cognizance, emotions and coping strategies. *Journal of Consumer Research*, Vol. 25, pp. 123–43.

Moschis, G.P. (2007), Stress and consumer behavior. *Journal of the Academy of Marketing Science*, Vol. 35 No. 3, pp. 430–44.

O'Guinn, T.C., and Faber, R.J. (1989), Compulsive buying: A phenomenological exploration. *Journal of Consumer Research*, Vol. 16 No. 2, pp. 147–57.

Pearlin, L. (1983), "Role strains and personal stress", in Kaplan, H.B. (ed.), *Psychosocial Stress: Trends in Theory and Research*, Academic Press, New York, pp. 3–30.

Pearlin, L.I. (1989), The sociological study of stress. *Journal of Health and Social Behavior*, Vol. 30 No. 3, pp. 241–56.

Reisch, L.A. (2001), Time and wealth. *Time & Society*, Vol. 10 Nos. 2–3, pp. 367–385.

Sapolsky, R.M. (2004), *Why Zebras Don't Get Ulcers: The Acclaimed Guide to Stress, Stress-Related Diseases, and Coping – Now Revised and Updated*, Macmillan, New York.

Sujan, M., Sujan, H., Bettman, J., and Verhallen, T.M. (1999), Sources of consumers' stress and their coping strategies. *European Advances in Consumer Research*, Vol. 4, pp. 182–7.

Sullivan, O. (2008), Busyness, status distinction and consumption strategies of the income rich, time poor. *Time & Society*, Vol. 17 No. 1, pp. 5–26.

Thoits, P.A. (1995), Stress, coping, and social support processes: Where are we? What next? *Journal of Health and Social Behavior*, Vol. 35, pp. 53–79.

Tuch, A.N., Bargas-Avila, J.A., Opwis, K., and Wilhelm, F.H. (2009), Visual complexity of websites: Effects on users' experience, physiology, performance, and memory. *International Journal of Human-Computer Studies*, Vol. 67 No. 9, pp. 703–15.

Turnbull, P.W., Leek, S., and Ying, G. (2000), Customer confusion: The mobile phone market. *Journal of Marketing Management*, Vol. 16 No. 1–3, pp. 143–63.

van Rompay, T.J.L., Tanja-Dijkstra, K., Verhoeven, J.W.M., and van Es, A.F. (2012), On store design and consumer motivation. *Environment and Behavior*, Vol. 44 No. 6, pp. 800–20.

Währborg, P. (2002), *Stress och den nya ohälsan*, Natur och kultur, Stockholm.

Warde, A. (1994), Consumption, identity-formation and uncertainty. *Sociology*, Vol. 28 No. 4, pp. 877–98.

Weiner, H. (1990), "Behavioral biology of stress and psychosomatic medicine", in Brown, M.R., Koob, G.F., and Rivier, C. (eds.), *Stress: Neurobiology and Neuroendocrinology*, Dekker, New York, pp. 23–51.

Woodward, I. (2006), Investigating consumption anxiety thesis: Aesthetic choice, narrativisation and social performance. *The Sociological Review*, Vol. 54 No. 2, pp. 263–82.

Yakhlef, A. (2015), Customer experience within retail environments: An embodied, spatial approach. *Marketing Theory*, Vol. 15 No. 4, pp. 545–64.

Part 2

Affluent marketplace stressors

4 Environmental marketplace stressors

"Too much perceptual input"

Environmental marketplace stressors are strains produced by the physical or online marketplace environment, i.e. strains that are external to the consumer body. Literature suggests that the information-rich affluent marketplace (Bawden and Robinson, 2009; Elliott, 2004; Eppler and Mengis, 2004; Jacoby et al., 1974; Malhotra, 1982; Scammon, 1977) provides environmental strains (Moschis, 2007; Pearlin, 1989; Sapolsky, 2004). Further it is suggested that these environmental strains are connected to "too much stimuli input" in relation to product offerings (Eppler and Mengis, 2004; Jacoby, 1984; Malhotra, 1984).

Perceptual overload

Perceptual overload as an environmental stressor in the affluent marketplace is related to consumers' perceptual capacities and sensory experiences. The literature recognizes that consumer information overload exists in affluent marketplaces (Bawden and Robinson, 2009; Jacoby et al., 1974; Malhotra, 1982; Mitchell et al., 2005). Information overload is commonly described as "receiving too much information" and is defined by marketing scholars as occurring when information supply exceeds the limits of human information-processing capacities (Eppler and Mengis, 2004; Jacoby et al., 1974; Malhotra, 1982; Scammon, 1977). The inherent frequency of product launches or product updates that are communicated in the physical affluent marketplace or via media – in which both product characteristics and the frequency with which products are launched are impossible to predict or control for shoppers – enhances the extent to which product-related information is experienced as a strain (Moschis, 2007; Pearlin, 1989; Sapolsky, 2004). Studies on information overload in an organizational context specify characteristics of information as levels of uncertainty, ambiguity, novelty, complexity and intensity, with implications for information-processing capacity and hence informational overload (Schneider, 1987). In consumer research, information overload has been approached primarily in terms of intensity and complexity and as a consumer decision quality problem. Information overload in the consumption context has been studied in relation to the use of relevant information (Jacoby et al., 1977), time to process information (Jacoby, 1984) and consumer decision adequacy (Malhotra, 1982). There is a lack of empirical evidence on information overload in various marketplace contexts. Studies on information overload in on-line consumption settings provide some insights (Chen et al., 2009; Lee and Lee, 2004). Perceived information overload, choice accuracy and subjective states in experiments of on-line buying of mobile phones and portable CD players have been measured. The results of these studies indicate that there are threshold levels regarding the number of alternatives consumers can process without reporting feelings of overload. As predicted, a relationship between information quantity and perceived information overload (supportive of Malhotra, 1982) has been confirmed (Chen et al., 2009; Lee and Lee, 2004). The results show that consumers who are overloaded with information are less satisfied, less confident and more confused (Lee and Lee, 2004).

From an embodied stress perspective, this evidence of information overload related to cognitive capacity when choosing products in a shopping context, is complemented by scientific accounts of overload connected to shoppers' sensory experiences. Seeing and touching merchandise as well as listening to in-store music and advertisements contribute to potential perceptual overload. Stimuli-rich physical marketplaces where "design features alongside human aspects, such as the physical dimensions, spatial layout, scent, odour, colour, music and other customers as well as service providers", provide consumer bodies with sensory experience (Yakhlef, 2015) and affect bodily arousal. Arousal was defined in Chapter 3 as "the neurophysiological basis underlying all processes in the human organism. Arousal is the basis of emotions, motivation, information processing, and behavioral reactions" (Bagozzi et al., 1999; Groeppel-Klein, 2005, p. 428). Arousal can vary from deep sleep to panic and reflects "the degree to which a person feels excited, stimulated, alert, or active in the situation" (Donovan and Rossiter, 1982, p. 38). We get aroused by our own internal reactions, i.e. our thought content or our emotions, or by external stimuli (Boucsein et al., 2001; Mehrabian and Russell, 1974). Arousal is connected to environmental strains in affluent marketplaces such as visual design features, including lightning, colour, product display, spatial arrangements and symbols, as well as scent and music, and these shape consumers' arousal levels (Bitner, 1992; Donovan and Rossiter, 1982; Garlin and Owen, 2006; Groeppel-Klein, 2005; Tuch et al.,

2009; Mehrabian and Russell, 1974; van Rompay et al., 2012; Kaltcheva and Weitz, 2006). Consumers' arousal levels are one bodily indication of reactions to marketplace stressors (Hubert and Kenning, 2008; van Rompay et al., 2012).

Retail researchers suggest that the totality of stimuli in retail environments determines the level of consumer bodily arousal (Bitner, 1992; Holahan, 1986). In addition, retail research proposes that information-rich and complex retail environments increase arousal (Berlyne, 1960; Mehrabian and Russell, 1974). One explanation is that retail environments are stimuli-intense, including many dissimilar stimuli elements that, in combination, cause higher arousal levels compared with other marketplaces (Berlyne, 1960; Groeppel-Klein, 2005; Tuch et al., 2009). A retail marketplace where "flashy colors, spotlights, visually striking price-tags, huge flat screens presenting movies, music, etc. . . . and novel, startling, or different stimuli arrangements (e.g. vivid-looking mannequins or unexpected decorations)" is the norm, is likely to cause highly aroused consumers (Groeppel-Klein, 2005, p. 430). High arousal levels produce perceptions of stress and information overload, regardless of whether they stem from positive or negative emotions (Donovan and Rossiter, 1982; Groeppel-Klein, 2005; van Rompay et al., 2012).

As discussed in Chapter 3, arousal as a construct is used to explain shopping behaviour (Babin et al., 1994; Groeppel-Klein, 2005), and the environmental strains of a stimuli-rich marketplace are linked to negative emotions related to choice uncertainty (Luce, 1998; Moschis, 2007), loss of control, frustration and increased consumer anxiety (Bawden and Robinson, 2009; Eppler and Mengis, 2004; Mitchell et al., 2005; Savolainen, 2007).

Opportunities to use media-mediated experiences

One particular dimension of the perceptual overload characteristic of the affluent marketplace is access to media-dependent accounts of product offerings distant in space and time. Lived experiences are immediate and largely non-reflexive, whereas mediated experiences are media-dependent accounts that enable the consumer to experience marketplace activities from a distance, through advertising, blogs etc. (Gadamer, 1989; Shankar et al., 2006). Thus, affluent consumers (can) experience the intense stimuli of the affluent marketplace when listening to the radio, surfing the internet, when watching TV etc. The large number of opportunities to experience the offerings of the marketplace – in other words, consumers' ability to experience media-dependent accounts of product offerings (e.g. advertising) that are separated from the marketplace in space and time

(Elliott, 2004) – provides intense sensory stimuli "in forms with which our senses, and prior experiences, are ill-equipped to deal" (Bawden and Robinson, 2009, p. 184). Research on on-line advertising shows that such advertising can contribute to consumer information overload (Hutter et al., 2013; McCoy et al., 2007).

In a study conducted by McCoy and colleagues (2007), the perceived intrusion by in-line ads was compared with that of pop-up/pop-under windows. In-line ads are commonly referred to as advertising that appears on your screen (while you search for information or read) in the form keywords that are matched with advertising text and/or related information (https://en.wikipedia.org/wiki/In-text_advertising). The results show that pop-up/pop-under advertising was 24% and 33% more intrusive respectively than in-line advertising in terms of effects on memory retention. These results were explained with reference to consumer attention disruption, which is hypothesized to limit information retrieval and processing (Festinger and Maccoby, 1964). However, from an embodied stress perspective, these results can purposefully be interpreted as caused by the incontrollable and unpredictable appearance of pop-up/pop-under advertising, As discussed in Chapter 3, consumers' ability to control and predict marketplace potential strains is decisive in determining if, and to what degree, such potential strains will be perceived as stressful by individual consumers (Moschis, 2007; Pearlin, 1989; Sapolsky, 2004). Thus, in the case of pop-ups and pop-unders, which by default cannot be controlled or predicted, it is highly probable that the use of such on-line advertising techniques will add to perceptual overload in affluent marketplaces.

Information overload as related to social media usage is investigated in organizational settings (Bucher et al., 2013), in relation to consumers' use of information technology (Venkatesh et al., 2012), as part of branding techniques (Goasduff and Pettey, 2011; Nielsen, 2011) and as a determinant of social media fatigue (Bright et al., 2015). Social media fatigue is defined as "a user's tendency to back away from social media participation when s/he becomes overwhelmed with information" (Bright et al., 2015, p. 149). These studies provide ample evidence that the advent of social media contributes to consumer information overload, defined as when the level of information received exceeds human information processing capacity (Jacoby et al., 1974). Social media as one type of marketplace-mediated experience adds to consumers' informational overload through interaction with companies and brands as well as interpersonal communication that fuels socially desirable consumption (see Chapter 5). Studies on social media-dependent information overload recognize the impact of such overload on well-being, loss of control and subsequent stress (Bucher et al., 2013).

Perceptual overload as a chronic affluent consumer role strain

The phenomenology of perception on which this book is based assumes that human experience occurs where the body (including the mind), the physical world and the social world meet (Merleau-Ponty, 1962). Building on this assumption, bodily experience is regarded as spontaneous, following our body schemas (Gallagher, 2005; Yakhlef, 2015). From an embodied stress perspective, information-based consumer overload cannot be separated from stimuli overload of the senses. A stress theory perspective implies that consumer perceptual overload represents a chronic role strain influenced by social and structural arrangements, such as the market in which shoppers are embedded (Pearlin, 1989). Chronic stressors – strains – are intimately connected to social roles and emphasize the link between people's well-being and socio-cultural contexts (Aneshensel, 1992; Pearlin, 1989). Consumer perceptual overload corresponds to one type of chronic role strain, role overload, that is described in sociological stress research (Pearlin, 1983, 1989). Role overload – when the demands on individuals' energy exceed their capacity within a specific role – is a condition that reflects the chronic overload properties of affluent marketplaces.

Marketing perspectives and perceptual overload

Affluent Western marketplaces and cultures of consumption are heavily shaped by marketing practice. From the embodied stress perspective taken in this book, two contemporary marketing perspectives – experiential and collaborative – contribute to experiences of perceptual overload in affluent marketplaces (Cova and Cova, 2012). Within the experiential marketing approach, firms compete on how to create positive emotional consumer experiences through branding (Pine and Gilmore, 1999; Schmitt, 1999, 2003). The logic of difference for firms from an experiential marketing perspective is provided by consumers' experiential immersion in the brands of the firm. Thus events, social media networking activities and advertising campaigns aim to stimulate consumers' sensory and emotional experiences. The collaborative marketing perspective implies less of management of consumers' emotional immersion and more management of co-creation meaning processes, even though experience marketing is a central feature within both marketing paradigms (Cova and Cova, 2012; Vargo and Lusch, 2008; Tynan and McKechnie, 2009). From a collaborative marketing perspective, firms compete on being considered authentic symbolic resources in consumers' meaning creation processes (Duncan and Moriarty, 1998; Holt, 2002). Both experiential and collaborative marketing approaches build on affecting consumers' experience as a marketing strategy. From an embodied stress perspective, firms' active management of consumers' marketplace experiences can potentially be perceived as stressful by consumers.

Holt (2002) describes how the rise of postmodern branding techniques and consumer culture are intertwined and how marketing strategists in our postmodern area weave brands into cultural communities such as ethnic subcultures, sports communities, professional communities etc. For example, by linking a specific brand to a specific sport community, the arenas in which consumers interact with brands increase, and these arenas are interactive. Such branding techniques are examples of the creation of human experience as occurring where the consumer body (including the mind), the physical world (for example a sports competition site) and the social world (the community) meet (Merleau-Ponty, 1962). Event marketing is one particular version of the use of events for branding purposes. Event marketing is considered as an effective marketing tool, as "nothing is more convincing than personal experiences" (Nickel, 1998). Event marketing creates new brand-related realities by staging marketing-events with which consumers interact which result in an emotional attachment to the brand (Zanger and Sistenich, 1996)" (Wohlfeil and Whelan, 2005, p. 181). Experiential marketing approaches, including event marketing, exemplify how firms' efforts to affect affluent consumer experiences are intensified and expanded in space, and that such marketing approaches aim to provide brand value by offering sensory meaning through sound, touch, sight, taste and smell (Tynan and McKechnie, 2009; Schmitt, 1999). The consumer body thus experiences the marketplace and its offerings not only at the point of purchase, but across a range of cultural contexts from sport competitions to music festivals and political manifestations. From an embodied stress framework, such widening of the affluent marketplace to include areas formerly not regarded as "commercial" has implications for consumers' perceived marketplace-induced stress.

Co-creation of value as a collaborative marketing strategy implies that consumption experiences are shared and that the value of specific brands is created in interaction with peers (Cova and Cova, 2012; Tynan and McKechnie, 2009). Marketing strategists increasingly work with social media platforms to stage consumer experiences, such that "the virtual world's mediated experiences stand alongside the real world's lived experiences as part of experience marketing" (Tynan and McKechnie, 2009). The internet has facilitated the formation of brand communities (Kozinets, 1999). The mediated experiences of the affluent marketplace enabled by social media increase the frequency and intensity of sensory stimuli and information related to product offerings. It is therefore highly probable that collaborative marketing techniques are linked to perceptual overload as a chronic affluent consumer role strain.

Bibliography

Aneshensel, C.S. (1992), Social stress: Theory and research. *Annual review of sociology*, Vol. 18 No. 1, pp. 15–38.

Babin, B.J., Darden, W.R., and Griffin, M. (1994), Work and/or fun: Measuring hedonic and utilitarian shopping value. *Journal of Consumer Research*, Vol. 20 No. 4, pp. 644–56.

Bagozzi, R.P., Gopinath, M., and Nyer, P.U. (1999), The role of emotions in marketing. *Journal of the Academy of Marketing Science*, Vol. 27 No. 2, pp. 184–206.

Bawden, D., and Robinson, L. (2009), The dark side of information: Overload, anxiety and other paradoxes and pathologies. *Journal of Information Science*, Vol. 35 No. 2, pp. 180–91.

Berlyne, D.E. (1960), *Conflict, arousal, and curiosity*, McGraw-Hill, New York.

Bitner, M.J. (1992), Servicescapes: The impact of physical surroundings on customers and employees. *Journal of Marketing*, Vol. 56 No. 2, pp. 57–71.

Boucsein, K., Weniger, G., Mursch, K., Steinhoff, B.J., and Irle, E. (2001), Amygdala lesion in temporal lobe epilepsy subjects impairs associative learning of emotional facial expressions. *Neuropsychologia*, Vol. 39 No. 3, pp. 231–6.

Bright, L.F., Kleiser, S.B., and Grau, S.L. (2015), Too much Facebook? An exploratory examination of social media fatigue. *Computers in Human Behavior*, Vol. 44, pp. 148–55.

Bucher, E., Fieseler, C., and Suphan, A. (2013), The stress potential of social media in the workplace. *Information, Communication & Society*, Vol. 31 No. 10, pp. 1639–67.

Chen, Y.C., Shang, R.A., and Kao, C.Y. (2009), The effects of information overload on consumers' subjective state towards buying decision in the internet shopping environment. *Electronic Commerce Research and Applications*, Vol. 8 No. 1, pp. 48–58.

Cova, B., and Cova, V. (2012), On the road to prosumption: Marketing discourse and the development of consumer competencies. *Consumption Markets & Culture*, Vol. 15 No. 2, pp. 149–68.

Donovan, R.J., and Rossiter, J.R. (1982), Store atmosphere: An environmental psychology approach. *Journal of Retailing*, Vol. 58 No. 1, pp. 34–57.

Duncan, T., and Moriarty, S.E. (1998), A communication-based marketing model for managing relationships. *The Journal of Marketing*, pp. 1–13.

Elliott, R. (2004), "Making up people: Consumption as a symbolic vocabulary for the construction of identity", in Ekström, K.M., and Brembeck, H. (eds.), *Elusive Consumption*, Berg Publishers, Oxford, pp. 11–25.

Eppler, M.J., and Mengis, J. (2004), The concept of information overload: A review of literature from organization science, accounting, marketing, MIS, and related disciplines. *Information Society*, Vol. 20 No. 5, pp. 325–44.

Festinger, L., and Maccoby, M. (1964), On resistance to persuasive communications. *Journal Abnormal and Social Psychology*, Vol. 68, pp. 359–66.

Gadamer, H.G. (1989), Truth and method (J. Weinsheimer & DG Marshall, trans.). *New York: Continuum*.

Gallagher, S. (2005), *How the Body Shapes the Mind*, Oxford University Press, New York.

Garlin, F.V., and Owen, K. (2006), Setting the tone with the tune: A meta-analytic review of the effects of background music in retail settings. *Journal of Business Research*, Vol. 59 No. 6, pp. 755–64.

Goasduff, L., and Pettey, C. (2011), *Gartner Survey Highlights Consumer Fatigue With Social Media*, www.gartner.com/it/page.jsp?id=1766814

Groeppel-Klein, A. (2005), Arousal and consumer in-store behavior. *Brain Research Bulletin*, Vol. 67 No. 5, pp. 428–37.

Holahan, C.J. (1986), Environmental psychology. *Annual review of psychology*, Vol. 37 No. 1, pp. 381–407.

Holt, D.B. (2002), Why do brands cause trouble? A dialectical theory of consumer culture and branding. *Journal of Consumer Research*, Vol. 29 No. 1, pp. 70–90.

Hubert, M., and Kenning, P. (2008), A current overview of consumer neuroscience. *Journal of Consumer Behaviour*, Vol. 7 No. 4–5, pp. 272–92.

Hutter, K., Hautz, J., Dennhardt, S., and Füller, J. (2013), The impact of user interactions in social media on brand awareness and purchase intention: The case of MINI on Facebook. *Journal of Product & Brand Management*, Vol. 22 No. 5/6, pp. 342–51.

Jacoby, J. (1984), Perspectives on information overload. *Journal of Consumer Research*, Vol. 10 No. 4, pp. 432–5.

Jacoby, J., Speller, D.E., and Kohn, C.A. (1974), Brand choice behavior as a function of information load. *Journal of Marketing Research*, Vol. 11 No. 1, pp. 63–9.

Jacoby, J., Szybillo, G.J., and Busato-Schach, J. (1977), Information acquisition behavior in brand choice situations. *Journal of Consumer Research*, Vol. 3 No. 4, pp. 209–16.

Kaltcheva, V.D., and Weitz, B.A. (2006), When should a retailer create an exciting store environment? *Journal of Marketing*, Vol. 70 No. 1, pp. 107–18.

Kozinets, R.V. (1999), E-tribalized marketing: The strategic implications of virtual communities of consumption. *European Management Journal*, Vol. 17 No. 3, pp. 252–64.

Lang, A. (2000), The limited capacity model of mediated message processing. *Journal of Communication* (Winter), pp. 46–70.

Lee, B.-K., and Lee, W.-N. (2004), The effect of information overload on consumer choice quality in an on-line environment. *Psychology and Marketing*, Vol. 21 No. 3, pp. 159–83.

Luce, M.F. (1998), Choosing to avoid: Coping with negatively emotion-laden consumer decisions. *Journal of Consumer Research*, Vol. 24 No. 4, pp. 409–33.

Malhotra, N.K. (1982), Information load and consumer decision making. *Journal of Consumer Research*, Vol. 8 No. 4, pp. 419–30.

Malhotra, N.K. (1984), Reflections on the information overload paradigm in consumer decision making. *Journal of Consumer Research*, Vol. 10 No. 4, pp. 436–40.

McCoy, S., Everard, A., Polak, P., and Galletta, D.F. (2007), The effects of online advertising. *Communications of the ACM*, Vol. 50 No. 3, pp. 84–8.

Mehrabian, A., and Russell, J.A. (1974), *An Approach to Environmental Psychology*, MIT Press, Cambridge, MA.

Merleau-Ponty, M. (1962), *Phenomenology of Perception*, Routledge, London.

Mitchell, V.W., Walsh, G., and Yamin, M. (2005), *Towards a Conceptual Model of Consumer Confusion*, NA-Advances in Consumer Research, Volume 32.

Moschis, G.P. (2007), Stress and consumer behavior. *Journal of the Academy of Marketing Science*, Vol. 35 No. 3, pp. 430–44.

Nickel, O. (1998), "Event: Ein neues Zauberwort?", in Nickel, O. (ed.), *Eventmarketing: Grundlagen und Erfolgsbeispiele*, Vahlen, München, pp. 3–12.

Nielsen. (2011), *State of Social Media: Social Media Report Q3*, www.nielsen.com/us/en/insights/reports/2011/social-media-report-q3.html, accessed September 10, 2011.

Pearlin, L. (1983), "Role strains and personal stress", in Kaplan, H.B. (ed.), *Psychosocial Stress: Trends in Theory and Research*, Academic Press, New York, pp. 3–30.

Pearlin, L.I. (1989), The sociological study of stress. *Journal of Health and Social Behavior*, Vol. 30 No. 3, pp. 241–56.

Pine, B.G., and Gilmore, J.J. (1999), *The Experience Economy*, Harvard Business Press, Boston, MA.

Sapolsky, R.M. (2004), *Why Zebras Don't Get Ulcers: The Acclaimed Guide to Stress, Stress-Related Diseases, and Coping – Now Revised and Updated*, Macmillan, New York.

Savolainen, R. (2007), Filtering and withdrawing: Strategies for coping with information overload in everyday contexts. *Journal of Information Science*, Vol. 33 No. 5, pp. 611–21.

Scammon, D.L. (1977), Information load and consumers. *Journal of Consumer Research*, Vol. 4 No. 3, pp. 148–55.

Schmitt, B. (1999), Experiential marketing. *Journal of Marketing Management*, Vol. 15 No. 1–3, pp. 53–67. doi:10.1362/026725799784870496.

Schmitt, B. (2003), *Customer Experience Management: A Revolutionary Approach to Connecting With Your Customers*, John Wiley & Sons, Hoboken, NJ.

Schneider, S.C. (1987), Information overload: Causes and consequences. *Human Systems Management*, Vol. 7 No. 2, pp. 143–53.

Shankar, A., Whittaker, J., and Fitchett, J.A. (2006), Heaven knows I'm miserable now. *Marketing Theory*, Vol. 6 No. 4, pp. 485–505.

Tuch, A.N., Bargas-Avila, J.A., Opwis, K., and Wilhelm, F.H. (2009), Visual complexity of websites: Effects on users' experience, physiology, performance, and memory. *International Journal of Human-Computer Studies*, Vol. 67 No. 9, pp. 703–15.

Tynan, C., and McKechnie, S. (2009), Experience marketing: A review and reassessment. *Journal of Marketing Management*, Vol. 25 No. 5–6, pp. 501–17.

van Rompay, T.J.L., Tanja-Dijkstra, K., Verhoeven, J.W.M., and van Es, A.F. (2012), On store design and consumer motivation. *Environment and Behavior*, Vol. 44 No. 6, pp. 800–20.

Vargo, S.L., and Lusch, R.F. (2008), From goods to service (s): Divergences and convergences of logics. *Industrial Marketing Management*, Vol. 37 No. 3, pp. 254–9.

Venkatesh, V., Thong, J.Y., and Xu, X. (2012), Consumer acceptance and use of information technology: Extending the unified theory of acceptance and use of technology. *MIS Quarterly*, Vol. 36 No. 1, pp. 157–78.

Wohlfeil, M., and Whelan, S. (2005), Event-marketing as innovative marketing communications: Reviewing the German experience. *Journal of Customer Behaviour*, Vol. 4 No. 2, pp. 181–207.

Yakhlef, A. (2015), Customer experience within retail environments: An embodied, spatial approach. *Marketing Theory*, Vol. 15 No. 4, pp. 545–64.

Yip, B., Rowlinson, S., and Siu, O.L. (2008), Coping strategies as moderators in the relationship between role overload and burnout. *Construction Management and Economics*, Vol. 26 No. 8, pp. 871–82.

Zanger, C., and Sistenich, F. (1996), Eventmarketing: Bestandsaufnahme, Standortbestimmung und ausgewählte theoretische Ansätze zur Erklärung eines innovativen Kommunikationsinstruments. *Marketing – Zeitschrift für Forschung und Praxis*, Vol. 18 No. 4, pp. 233–42.

5 Internalized marketplace-induced stressors

"Idealized identity" overload

In line with the allostatic view on stress that stipulates that consumers can react to anticipated marketplace stressors based on prior experience (Sapolsky, 2004), internal and socially affluent marketplace-induced stressors are internalized social strains that represent learned culture-specific consumer perceptual capacities (Gallagher, 2005; Yakhlef, 2015). Internalized affluent marketplace-induced strains are intimately related to Western consumer culture. One example of such internalized marketplace stressors is the social norm of constantly partaking in consumption activities and adhering to Western affluent consumer culture ideals. Such norms are reflected in shopping motivated by emotional and identity-related benefits is linked to symbolic overload through countless possibilities of self-formation produced in the marketplace (Campbell, 2004; Elliott, 2004). In this context, the continuous redefinition of socially desirable fashion objects explains why the choice of clothes can be associated with considerable stress and anxiety (Dittmar, 2008; Halliwell et al., 2007; Luce, 1998; Moschis, 2007). Western consumer culture is not "a general force structuring consumer actions but, rather, is better understood as a skeletal metacultural logic centered on channeling desires and identities through consumer choices and actions that gets articulated in very different way across different markets" (Holt, 2012, p. 240). Thus the very core of consumer culture – identity-making through consumer choice – can be regarded as stressful (an internalized stressor) from an embodied stress perspective.

Continuous need for experiential input in individualized identity-making

Literature abounds with accounts of the consumption anxieties of choice in contemporary Western affluent consumer culture associated with the dismantling of traditional institutions and subsequent increased individual freedom (Bauman, 1998; Beck, 1992; Dittmar, 2008; Giddens, 1991; Halliwell and Dittmar, 2004; Halliwell et al., 2007; Kasser, 2002; Richins,

2013; Woodward, 2006). Individual and aspirational self-defining practices in Western consumer culture, as opposed to ascribed identities of the past, are characterized by self-discovery through monitoring emotional reactions to specific products and services (Campbell, 2004; Elliott, 1997). The assumption that personal experience, in the form of perceived needs and wants, alone "constitutes the highest authority" (Campbell, 2004, p. 87) has important implications for our understanding of affluent consumption. One main characteristic of liquid identity in Western consumer culture, where individualized and emotion-based identity-making is expressed in consumption, is the central role of emotion and desire, rather than reason and rationality, in self-defining processes (Elliott, 2004). The central role of emotion and desire, paired with individualization and subsequent moulding of identity and ideology, produces a continuous need for experiential input (Cherrier et al., 2012; Elliott, 2004; Jantzen et al., 2012; Mikkonen et al., 2014), which is provided in the affluent marketplace.

Individualized and emotion-based identity-making has consequences for why and how the affluent marketplace is perceived as stressful by consumers, in particular when it comes to internal and social stressors. First, emotion-based identity-making implies a continuous need for new stimuli that provide ontological reassurance, e.g. "I feel therefore I am" (Campbell, 2004); these stimuli are readily produced by the affluent marketplace in the production of sensory experiences that are potential stressors, as described in Chapter 4. The rich arsenal of symbols produced in this marketplace and conveyed by advertising further fuels the desire and imagination of consumers, and is regarded as the main resource for identity-making and maintenance (Arnould and Thompson, 2005; Campbell, 1987; Elliott, 2004). Second, many affluent consumption practices take on primary existential meanings as "we try to resolve our sense of the profound gulf between the striving for personalization and individuality in life and our consciousness of the crushing anonymity of death and global ubiquity" (Miller, 2009, p. 168). In other words, affluent consumption practices are intimately linked to "establishing normativity in kinship" (Clarke and Miller, 2002, p. 211). Internalized stress in the affluent consumption context is thus related to consumption anxiety as socially performed, i.e. "an emotion experienced by actors in the context of particular social settings in which presentations of self are called to account" (May, 1950; Woodward, 2006, p. 6). Internalized affluent marketplace-induced stressors connected to such social anxiety are discussed next.

Affluent consumption as kinship in practice

The definition of anxiety proposed by May half a century ago is concurrent with recent literature on identity and consumption (Woodward, 2006). The protection of identity and feelings of anxiety are intertwined, as "anxiety is the apprehension cued off by a *threat to some value* which the individual holds essential to his existence as a personality" (May,1950, p. 191). As described in Chapter 3, perceptions of threats to cultural and social values are inherently stressful. Thus, from an embodied perspective, affluent consumer anxiety related to identity-making is characterized as an internalized marketplace stressor.

Individualistic self-definition (identity-making) by means of emotional self-discovery is a crucial dimension of shopping practice, reflected in the understanding of shopping as anxious. In an ethnographic study of female shopping for clothes in London, Clarke and Miller (2002) found that buying new clothes is intimately linked to anxiety regarding "knowing what to like". For clothing, most individuals do not know what their taste is and are too anxious to choose what clothing to buy without social (family and friends) or institutional support (Clarke and Miller, 2002). They describe how Charmaigne, who has set out to buy a floral print garment:

> her mother and the researcher is a constant sounding board upon which to exchange opinions, with the sense that our approval might be seen as evidence against as for the garment in question. Even with all this support, the difficulty that was evident for Charmaigne, again and again, was knowing whether she actually liked a print or not and therefore being able to determine what her taste was or could be.
>
> (p. 197)

In addition to Charmaigne, who exhibits anxiety about what age her clothes signal – is she dressing "too childish" or should she pick clothing that makes her look more mature? – Clarke and Miller provide examples through the experience of Sharon and Katie. Sharon feels extremely let down by failures to dress appropriately, i.e. like friends and family at various parties, and Katie, for whom the failure to make headway in a career is manifested through redefining her style and wardrobe. Through these examples, Clarke and Miller conclude that anxiety in clothes shopping is a normal condition and comes in various forms.

As the examples of clothes shopping show and as explored in material culture studies, shopping for clothing and goods for the home can be described as "kinship in practice": i.e. who am I in relation to others, and how should I show who I am in terms of dress and interior design (Clarke, 2001; Clarke and Miller, 2002; McRobbie, 2008; Miller, 2001; Woodward, 2006). In this stream of research the same dialectic between the aspirational and actual that leads to restless and anxious searching for the normative in shopping for home decoration, as in clothes shopping (Clarke, 2001). Anxiety in this kind of affluent consumption practice is hence not restricted to addictive behaviours such as compulsive shopping. Instead, consumption practice is inherently linked to "establishing normativity in kinship" (Clarke and Miller, 2002, p. 211), a process of determining right and wrong in relation to important others. Thus, neither the home nor the wardrobe should be regarded as expressive; rather, consumption practice is a reflection of anxiety regarding relationships to other people. Woodward refines the concept of consumption anxiety in his study of home decoration to include not only aesthetic anxiety over having chosen the right colour but also a degree of anxiousness of being perceived as consumerist in a superficial way (Woodward, 2006).

One important outcome of these material culture studies is that they describe stress in contemporary (Western) society as produced by the existential task of making up our own moral rules (what Miller calls normativity) as a commoditized phenomenon (Miller, 2009). Consumption practice thus becomes a search for defining the normative through material culture. Consumption objects ease the existential burden of affluent consumers through the capacity of different consumption practice to reduce anxiety caused by contemporary stress on normativity (Clarke and Miller, 2002). This stress is contemporary in its character, as institutions (religion, family and other) no longer provide us with structural and structured moral guidelines and a conscience that is collective (Giddens, 1991). Instead, we must make up our own moral rules as individuals and try different approaches to kinship in the material sphere. It is this condition of modernity (Giddens, 1991) that Clarke and Miller (2002) refer to when they state that "almost any form of shopping can be understood in relation to the importance of establishing normativity in kinship" (p. 211).

The social and internal strain of fashion objects

From a stress perspective internalized marketplace-induced strains are closely related to the fashion object as the scene for temporarily stable but constantly changing idealized identities (Schiermer, 2011; Simmel, 1904). The fashion object spurs a dialectic process between aspirational and actual identity in consumption contexts. The literature describes the fashion object as providing two seemingly opposing social functions: individuality in a socially accepted manner, and distinction (Banister and Hogg, 2004; Cholachatpinyo et al., 2002; Gronow, 1997; Simmel, 1904; Sproles, 1974; Thompson and Haytko, 1997). Hence, the value of the fashion object is found in the logic of social competition and interaction. In this book the fashion object is understood as intimately related to individualized and commoditized identity-making in affluent Western consumer culture, which is an ideology of change that endorses buying new goods (Mikkonen et al., 2014; Moisander et al., 2010; Thompson and Haytko, 1997). Industries of fashion produce fashion objects (as opposed to the fashion industry, which is commonly restricted to clothing fashion) and are defined as those that offer products (fashion objects) that are subject to change, obsolescence, or replacement by new product versions, which are valued predominantly based on qualities other than functional utility, such as social acceptability and desirable taste (Alvesson, 2013; Sproles, 1974). Examples of industries of fashion are the automobile, clothing, furniture, electronics, home furnishings, household apparel and mobile phone industries. From an embodied perspective in which perception is a bodily activity, consumers experience fashion objects and their representations by means of learned perceptual skills that enable them to experience and relate to these objects with meanings of individuality and socially acceptable differences (Gallagher, 2005; Merleau-Ponty, 1962; Yakhlef, 2015). Consumer stress studies indicate that fashion objects are intimately connected to consumer role overload as a result of constantly changing market offerings (Luce, 1998; Moschis, 2007). Fashion objects that are continuously subject to change and valued/consumed for reasons of social competition provide consumer with ontological reassurance through experiential input (Campbell, 2004; Denegri-Knott and Molesworth, 2010; Elliott, 1997, 2004; Jantzen et al., 2012; Shankar et al., 2006). Hence, a constant supply of novel fashion objects within the context of the Western affluent consumer culture-oriented marketplace (where emotion and desire form the basis of identity), is performative in the sense that it provides consumer role overload. Socially valued novel fashion objects launched on the market imply that existing versions or models of the specific object are potentially considered threats to cultural and social values (Moschis, 2007; Pearlin, 1989; Sapolsky, 2004). Novel fashion objects as updated versions or new models entering the marketplace will contribute to shoppers' potential experience of threat-related emotions or thought content linked to earlier versions of the very same fashion objects. Thus, as novel fashion objects are launched, older or existing versions can be understood as social and internal marketplace-induced strains or stressors (Duhachek, 2005; Sujan et al., 1999). Fashion, as the mechanism that spurs constant re-definition of market-based identity-making in affluent consumer culture, adds to the stress produced by consumer perceptual overload described in Chapter 4 on two levels: information overload triggering emotional reactions per see (e.g. abundant range of alternatives to emotionally react to and choose from) and identity confusion that triggers a restless search for information cues regarding the "right outfit". The affluent marketplace is perceived as stressful as new product versions or collections create "a situation in which control has not been lost yet, even though such a threat is constantly present" (Luomala, 2002, p. 830), the situation in this case referring to identity-making by monitoring feelings and evaluating kinship vis-à-vis new products made available on the market. Such marketplace stress is illustrated by experiments on ideal model internalization for women and men where results indicate a "think ideal, feel bad" sequence, which is discussed next.

Think ideal, feel bad

Individualized and emotional-based identity-making performed primarily in the marketplace where idealized identity images are constantly being produced and communicated, leads to stress and anxiety (Dittmar, 2008; Halliwell et al., 2007; Kasser, 2002). Such anxiety is related to discrepancies between idealized material images and the body (Duhachek, 2005). In the affluent consumer culture context social acceptance is intimately linked to idealized identities continuously updated by fashion and media. Socially desirable consumption objects are represented in terms of idealized and often unrealistic ideals of the body, the family and of material standing (Dittmar, 2008). From an embodied perspective, such product representations teach and enable consumers in the affluent marketplace to understand consumption objects with meanings of individuality and socially acceptable differences. Psychological research clearly indicates that consumption objects represent highly desirable and often unattainable identities, which are mediated by advertising and produce experiences of low self-esteem, identity deficit and anxiety connected to dissatisfaction with our actual identity (Dittmar, 2008).

Few empirical studies have addressed consumption as an internalized strain in the context of Western consumer culture. However, psychological studies provide evidence that idealized and socially desired product-related images produce negative self-images and identity deficits among consumers through a "think ideal, feel bad" sequence (Dittmar, 2008). Idealized thin female or muscular male models lead women and men to feel anxious about their bodies as they compare themselves with the ideal portrayed by advertising (Halliwell and Dittmar, 2004; Halliwell et al., 2007). Self-representation or self-conceptualization is here regarded as an important part of the embodied self (Elliott, 2004; Entwistle, 2000). Building on self-discrepancy theory (Higgins, 1987), experiments in which exposure to advertisements of deodorants featuring idealized models – ultra-thin females in experiments with women and muscular V-shaped males in experiments with young men – were compared to exposure to deodorant ads without models (Halliwell and Dittmar, 2004; Halliwell et al., 2007). The results indicate that exposure to idealized models activated significantly stronger self-discrepancies – e.g. anxiety activated by thoughts focusing on the gap between their actual and ideal self in terms of thinness/being muscular – among women and men who had internalized the thin/muscular ideal compared to the control condition (non-internalized). The same "think ideal, feel bad" mechanism is suggested in peer culture through the pressure to have "cool" things or the right taste (Dittmar, 2008; McRobbie, 2008). In a study of social motives for wanting to have "cool things" among 183 children aged 8–11, it was found that children who perceive high levels of pressure to conform to peer culture "tend to subscribe to the view that having or not having certain material goods will have significant impacts on the quality of peer interactions and relationships" (Dittmar, 2008, p. 194). McRobbie's study of women and fashion consumption draws a picture of the "standard feature of women's lives to attempt to make 'correct choices' to prevent them from falling into 'the shadows' of a set of elitist social relations" (2008, p. 174). In the shopping context, the anxiety of idealized identity-making is one example of low self-esteem (Kasser, 2002). Self-esteem is commonly understood as based on people's evaluation of themselves and chronic discrepancies between the ideal and the actual is fuelled by aspirational images in advertising (Kasser, 2002). Summarizing the research evidence on identity discrepancies fuelled by idealized images in the marketplace, I propose that emotion-based identity-making in the Western consumer culture landscape is potentially stressful. The research evidence presented in this section provides arguments that anticipated and learned "think ideal, feel bad" sequences resulting from idealized product imaginary can be regarded as an important internalized affluent marketplace-induced stressor. The gap between actual and ideal identity is inherent to fashion, where products are valued mainly because their aspirational value (as they are new and desired by others). Hence, fashion marketplaces are stressful for affluent consumers in Western consumer cultures who mainly rely on product-related symbolic meanings as resources for identity-making.

Marketing practice and the governmentality of consumer desire

Studies on the governmentality of consumer desire describe how novel product versions in industries of fashion, such as smartphones, clothing and household apparel, suggest consumer identities and forms of identification through new product launches, branding and visual imagery (Moisander et al., 2010). The visual imaginary of product offerings in advertising and media influence consumers' understanding of these offerings by suggesting identities and forms of identification (Elliot and Leonard, 2004; Mikkonen et al., 2014; Peñaloza, 1998; Schroeder, 2002). Such advertising no doubt performs socially desirable needs for certain products that are considered "cool" or "trendy". Seasonal trends and frequent style modifications by means of launches of new collections that are heavily advertised as part of new, connected and up-to-date life-styles create desire in consumers to constantly update their arsenal of fashion objects (Moisander et al., 2010). Empirical studies suggest that marketplaces that are endowed with culturally valued continuous style updates trigger a restless search for information cues regarding the "right outfit" or the "right arsenal of products", indicating enduring consumer role-overload properties in novelty shopping (Clarke and Miller, 2002; McRobbie, 2008; Miller, 2001; Woodward, 2006).

Consumer anxiety and stress

"Think ideal, feel bad" sequences are, with the embodied approach of this book in mind, related to mood enhancement, self-assurance and identity support. Research on buying motives among ordinary buyers (non-compulsory buyers) strongly suggests that shopping in general is related to emotional and identity-related benefits as frequently as to functional motives (Dittmar, 2005). A four week shopping diary study (including personal consumer goods, excluding routine household goods) with ordinary and compulsory buyers clearly provides evidence for strong self-assuring motives of shopping for both groups, the differences only being a matter of degree (Dittmar, 2005). Dittmar's discussion of psychologically motivated shopping is highly informative to our understanding of anxiety and self-assurance in consumption of novel goods. Shopping motivated by mood enhancement is "as much about wanting to feel better about oneself, as about simply wanting to feel better" (Dittmar, 2008, p. 103), as mood is interlinked with identity and self-evaluation.

A stress perspective in general, and on internalized marketplace-induced stressors in particular, delivers a complementary understanding of the underpinnings of consumer anxiety reported in psychological and materialism studies (Halliwell and Dittmar, 2004; O'Guinn and Faber, 1989; Richins, 2013). As noted earlier, anxiety is predominantly understood as social anxiety in consumption literature, which is different from psychological and clinical anxieties (Leary, 1983). In particular, interpersonal evaluation is distinguished as a manifestation of social anxiety experienced in the arena of aesthetic and status-based consumption (Woodward, 2006). Consumer anxiety is generally investigated and understood as a negative cognitive valuation of feelings that involves the comparison of products or body parts with idealized models in advertising (Halliwell and Dittmar, 2004; O'Guinn and Faber, 1989; Richins, 2013). Such anxiety is described in terms of personal traits such as materialism (Belk, 1984; Richins and Dawson, 1992) or compensatory consumption (Woodruffe-Burton and Elliott, 2005). Investigations of consumer anxiety build on a cognitive tradition focused on negative threat-related thought content (Fishel, 2007). From the allostatic view of brain-coordinated bodily balance, stressors experienced by the body (including the mind) are automatically followed by reactions and efforts that seek to restore bodily equilibrium. Thus, in contrast to studies where anxiety is conceptualized in terms of certain personal traits or characteristic behaviours (such as materialism or compensatory consumption) a stress perspective assumes that the potentially stressful properties of the affluent marketplace can cause stress in each and every consumer's body (which includes the mind).

The stress theory framework suggests an alternative understanding of consumer anxiety. Descriptors such as desire, compensatory consumption and self-esteem dominate the contemporary scientific understanding of consumption anxiety. A stress perspective views desire (Belk et al., 2003), shopping for purposes of compensation of existential or social needs (Shrum et al., 2014; Woodruffe-Burton and Elliott, 2005) and the restoration of self-esteem (Burroughs et al., 2013) as the consequences of marketplace internal strains, which are individually represented, depending on individual circumstances and coping strategies. A stress perspective hence understands the cognition-based underpinnings of consumer desire as imaginative "cravings for consumer goods not yet possessed "(Belk et al., 2003, p. 174) and of compensatory consumption as threat-motivated consumption (Rucker and Galinsky, 2008; Shrum et al., 2014) along a continuous scale of perceived internal marketplace-induced strains. As an example, Belk et al.'s (2003) differentiation between compulsive consumption (which is one type of addictive compensatory consumption; see Woodruffe-Burton and Elliott, 2005 for an overview) and consumer desire based on different focal objects is contested on the basis of the proposed stress framework. Their argument is that the focal object of compulsive consumption is anxiety reduction and that the consumption object is secondary, whereas consumer desire is directed toward a particular desired and idealized object. These arguments can be questioned from an embodied stress position in which fashion objects are intimately connected to marketplace-induced strains, and individual reactions depend substantially on stress coping strategies (which will be discussed in detail in Chapter 9).

Bibliography

Alvesson, M. (2013), *The Triumph of Emptiness: Consumption, Higher Education, and Work Organization*, Oxford University Press, Oxford.

Arnould, E.J., and Thompson, C.J. (2005), Consumer Culture Theory (CCT): Twenty years of research. *Journal of Consumer Research*, Vol. 31 No. 4, pp. 868–82.

Banister, E.N., and Hogg, M.K. (2004), Negative symbolic consumption and consumers' drive for self-esteem: The case of the fashion industry. *European Journal of Marketing*, Vol. 38 No. 7, pp. 850–68.

Bauman, Z. (1998), *Work, Consumerism and the New Poor*, Open University Press, Berkshire, UK.

Beck, U. (1992), *Risk Society: Towards a New Modernity* (Vol. 17), Sage, London.

Belk, R.W. (1984), Cultural and historical differences in concepts of self and their effects on attitudes toward having and giving. *Advances in Consumer Research*, Vol. 11 No. 1, pp. 753–60.

Belk, R.W., Ger, G., and Askegaard, S. (2003), The fire of desire: A multisited inquiry into consumer passion. *Journal of Consumer Research*, Vol. 30 No. 3, pp. 326–51.

Burroughs, J.E., Chaplin, L.N., Pandelaere, M., Norton, M.I., Ordabayeva, N., Gunz, A., and Dinauer, L. (2013), Using motivation theory to develop a transformative consumer research agenda for reducing materialism in society. *Journal of Public Policy & Marketing*, Vol. 32 No. 1, pp. 18–31.

Campbell, C. (1987), *The Romantic Ethic and the Spirit of Modern Consumerism*, Blackwell, London.

Campbell, C. (2004), "I shop therefore I know that I am: The metaphysical basis of modern consumerism", in Ekström, K. and Brembeck, H. (eds.), *Elusive Consumption*, Berg Publishers, Oxford, pp. 27–44.

Cherrier, H., Szuba, M., and Özcaglar-Toulouse, N. (2012), Barriers to downward carbon emission: Exploring sustainable consumption in face of the glass floor. *Journal of Marketing Management*, Vol. 28 No. 3–4, pp. 397–419.

Cholachatpinyo, A., Fletcher, B., Padgett, I., and Crocker, M. (2002), A conceptual model of the fashion process – Part 1. *Journal of Fashion Marketing and Management: An International Journal*, Vol. 6 No. 1, pp. 11–23.

Clarke, A. (2001), "The aesthetics of social aspiration", in Miller, D. (ed.), *Home Possessions*, Berg Publishers, Oxford, pp. 23–47.

Clarke, A., and Miller, D. (2002), Fashion and anxiety. *Fashion Theory*, Vol. 6 No. 2, pp. 191–214.

Denegri-Knott, J., and Molesworth, M. (2010), 'Love it. Buy it. Sell it': Consumer desire and the social drama of eBay. *Journal of Consumer Culture*, Vol. 10 No. 1, pp. 56–79.

Dittmar, H. (2005), A new look at 'compulsive buying': Self – Discrepancies and materialistic values as predictors of compulsive buying tendency. *Journal of Social and Clinical Psychology*, Vol. 24 No. 6, pp. 806–33.

Dittmar, H. (2008), *Consumer Culture, Identity and Well-Being*, Psychology Press, New York.

Duhachek, A. (2005), Coping: A multidimensional, hierarchical framework of responses to stressful consumption episodes. *Journal of Consumer Research*, Vol. 32 No. 1, pp. 41–53.

Elliott, R. (1997), Existential consumption and irrational desire. *European Journal of Marketing*, Vol. 31 No. 3/4, pp. 285–96.

Elliott, R. (2004), "Making up people: Consumption as a symbolic vocabulary for the construction of identity", in Ekström, K.M., and Brembeck, H. (eds.), *Elusive Consumption*, Berg Publishers, Oxford, pp. 11–25.

Elliot, R., and Leonard, C. (2004), Peer pressure and poverty: Exploring fashion brands and consumption symbolism among children of the British poor. *Journal of Consumer Behavior*, Vol. 3, pp. 347–59.

Entwistle, J. (2000), Fashion and the fleshy body: Dress as embodied practice. *Fashion Theory*, Vol. 4 No. 3, pp. 323–47.

Fishel, M.N. (2007), *Cognitive Content Specificity of Test Anxiety and Depression in College Women*, ProQuest, Ann Arbor, MI.

Gallagher, S. (2005), *How the Body Shapes the Mind*, Oxford University Press, New York.

Giddens, A. (1991), *Modernity and Self-Identity: Self and Society in the Late Modern Age*, Polity Press, Cambridge.

Gronow, J. (1997), *The Sociology of Taste*, Routledge, London.

Halliwell, E., and Dittmar, H. (2004), Does size matter? The impact of model's body size on advertising effectiveness and women's body-focused anxiety. *Journal of Social and Clinical Psychology*, Vol. 23 No. 1, pp. 104–22.

Halliwell, E., Dittmar, H., and Orsborn, A. (2007), The effects of exposure to muscular male models among men: Exploring the moderating role of gym use and exercise motivation. *Body Image*, Vol. 4 No. 3, pp. 278–87.

Higgins, E.T. (1987), Self-discrepancy: A theory relating self and affect. *Psychological Review*, Vol. 94 No. 3, pp. 319–40.

Holt, D.B. (2012), Constructing sustainable consumption: From ethical values to the cultural transformation of unsustainable markets. *The Annals of the American Academy of Political and Social Science*, Vol. 644 No. 1, pp. 236–55.

Jantzen, C., Fitchett, J., Østergaard, P., and Vetner, M. (2012), Just for fun? The emotional regime of experiential consumption. *Marketing Theory*, Vol. 12 No. 2, pp. 137–54.

Kasser, T. (2002), *The High Price of Materialism*, MIT Press, Cambridge, MA.

Leary, M.R. (1983), *Understanding social anxiety: Social, personality and clinical perspectives*, Vol. 153. Sage Publications, Inc.

Luce, M.F. (1998), Choosing to avoid: Coping with negatively emotion-laden consumer decisions. *Journal of Consumer Research*, Vol. 24 No. 4, pp. 409–33.

Luomala, H.T. (2002), An empirical analysis of the practices and therapeutic power of mood-alleviative consumption in Finland. *Psychology and Marketing*, Vol. 19 No. 10, pp. 813–36.

May, R. (1950), *The Meaning of Anxiety*, The Ronald Press Company, New York.

McRobbie, A. (2008), Young women and consumer culture. *Cultural Studies*, Vol. 22 No. 5, pp. 531–50.

Merleau-Ponty, M. (1962), *Phenomenology of Perception*, Routledge, London.

Mikkonen, I., Vicdan, H., and Markkula, A. (2014), What not to wear? Oppositional ideology, fashion, and governmentality in wardrobe self-help. *Consumption Markets & Culture*, Vol. 17 No. 3, pp. 254–73.

Miller, D. (2001), "Behind closed doors", in Miller, D. (ed.), *Home Possessions: Material Culture Behind Closed Doors*, Berg, Oxford, pp. 1–23.

Miller, D. (2009), "Buying time", in Shove, E., Trentmann, F., and Wilk, R. (eds.), *Time, Consumption and Everyday Life: Practice, Materiality and Culture*, Berg, Oxford, pp. 157–70.

Moisander, J., Markkula, A., and Eräranta, K. (2010), Construction of consumer choice in the market: Challenges for environmental policy. *International Journal of Consumer Studies*, Vol. 34 No. 1, pp. 73–9.

Moschis, G.P. (2007), Stress and consumer behavior. *Journal of the Academy of Marketing Science*, Vol. 35 No. 3, pp. 430–44.

O'Guinn, T.C., and Faber, R.J. (1989), Compulsive buying: A phenomenological exploration. *Journal of Consumer Research*, pp. 147–57.

Pearlin, L.I. (1989), The sociological study of stress. *Journal of Health and Social Behavior*, Vol. 30 No. 3, pp. 241–56.

Peñaloza, L. (1998), Just doing it: A visual ethnographic study of spectacular consumption behavior at Nike Town. *Consumption, Markets & Culture*, Vol. 2, pp. 337–465.

Richins, M.L. (2013), When wanting is better than having: Materialism, transformation expectations, and product-evoked emotions in the purchase process. *Journal of Consumer Research*, Vol. 40 No. 1, pp. 1–18.

Richins, M.L., and Dawson, S. (1992), A consumer values orientation for materialism and its measurement: Scale development and validation. *Journal of Consumer Research*, Vol. 19 No. 3, pp. 303–16.

Rucker, D.D., and Galinsky, A.D. (2008), Desire to acquire: Powerlessness and compensatory consumption. *Journal of Consumer Research*, Vol. 35 No. 2, pp. 257–67.

Sapolsky, R.M. (2004), *Why Zebras Don't Get Ulcers: The Acclaimed Guide to Stress, Stress-Related Diseases, and Coping – Now Revised and Updated*, Macmillan, New York.

Schiermer, B. (2011), Quasi-objects, cult objects and fashion objects: On two kinds of fetishism on display in modern culture. *Theory, Culture & Society*, Vol. 28 No. 1, pp. 81–102.

Schroeder, J.E. (2002), *Visual Consumption*, Routledge, London.

Shankar, A., Whittaker, J., and Fitchett, J.A. (2006), Heaven knows I'm miserable now. *Marketing Theory*, Vol. 6 No. 4, pp. 485–505.

Shrum, L.J., Lowrey, T.M., Pandelaere, M., Ruvio, A.A., Gentina, E., Furchheim, P., Herbert, M., Hudders, L., Lens, I., Mandel, N., Nairn, A., Samper, A., Soscia, I., and Steinfield, L. (2014), Materialism: The good, the bad, and the ugly. *Journal of Marketing Management*, Vol. 30 No. 17–18, pp. 1858–81.

Simmel, G. (1904), Fashion. *International Quarterly*, Vol. 10, pp. 130–55.

Sproles, G.B. (1974), "Fashion theory: A conceptual framework", in Ward, S. and Wright, P. (eds.), *NA – Advances in Consumer Research* (Vol. 1), Association for Consumer Research, Ann Abor, MI, pp. 463–72.

Sujan, M., Sujan, H., Bettman, J., and Verhallen, T. (1999), "Sources of consumers' stress and their coping strategies", in Dubois, B., Lowrey, T., and Shrum, L. (eds.), *European Advances in Consumer Research* (Vol. 4), Association for Consumer Research, Provo, UT, pp. 182–7.

Thompson, C.J., and Haytko, D.L. (1997), Speaking of fashion: Consumers' uses of fashion discourses and the appropriation of countervailing cultural meanings. *Journal of Consumer Research*, Vol. 24 No. 1, pp. 15–42.

Woodruffe-Burton, H., and Elliott, R. (2005), Compensatory consumption and narrative identity theory. *Advances in Consumer Research*, Vol. 32 No. 1, pp. 461–5.

Woodward, I. (2006), Investigating consumption anxiety thesis: Aesthetic choice, narrativisation and social performance. *The Sociological Review*, Vol. 54 No. 2, pp. 263–82.

Yakhlef, A. (2015), Customer experience within retail environments: An embodied, spatial approach. *Marketing Theory*, Vol. 15 No. 4, pp. 545–64.

6 Structural life-style stressors
"Work and consumption rich, time poor"

This chapter outlines affluent marketplace-induced structural stressors. Such structural strains, or stressors, relate in various ways to the intimate connection recognized and described by Swedish economist Linder (1970) between consumers' time allocation and income. This chapter builds on research relevant for "work/consumption rich, time poor" affluent consumption life-styles. The structural features of affluent marketplace stressors are deeply connected to the environmental and internalized stressors described in Chapters 4 and 5. The elaboration of the structural properties of these marketplace-induced stressors enable us to see clearly the common denominator of affluent consumer strains by zooming out and focusing on affluent consumer group characteristics that have an impact on sustainable consumption.

"Work/consumption rich, time poor" affluence

In Chapter 1, affluent consumption in the Western consumer culture context was defined as *the financial possibility to consume in accordance with socially desirable consumption (fashion) trends*. This definition acknowledges that (large) groups of affluent consumers, though not all, engage in unsustainable consumption practices as these practices require large inputs of resources and energy. The literature proposes that affluent consumers characterized as "work/consumption rich, time poor" face marketplace-induced stressors that are related to the time structures of the "work/consumption rich, time poor" affluent life-style.

"Work/consumption rich, time poor" structural features were discussed by Linder (1970). His theory on time allocation provides input to sustainable consumption studies, in particular those focusing on the seemingly automatic growth in consumption that follows from increased disposable income (Sanne, 2002; Röpke, 2009). One important question related to rising affluence, time allocation and sustainability is "Why are productivity increases transformed relatively more into income increases instead of leisure in the postwar years?" (Röpke, 2009, p. 403). According to Linder's neoclassical theory, the answer to this question would be that consumers maximize utility, or yield, per unit of their time. Hence, consumers theoretically spend their time working or at leisure, depending on their income level. Time and consumer goods are regarded as substitutable in generating yield; thus, as income rises, we profit from spending more time working and spending our increased income on goods and using less leisure time. As we become more affluent, we work more and have less leisure time, resulting in an intensification of leisure and high-materials/energy intensive consumption (Devetter and Rousseau, 2011; Röpke, 2009; Schor, 1991; Southerton, 2003; Knight et al., 2013). For example, work rich, time poor households use faster transportation, which usually implies higher GHG emissions, to save time (Knight et al., 2013).

Linder's perspective, in which time is intertwined with income and gains in productivity are used for increased consumption instead of increased leisure time, has been developed by Schor (1991) and is deeply problematic from a sustainability perspective (Jalas, 2002; Reisch, 2001; Röpke, 2009). From Linder's perspective, increasing affluence is linked to time shortages. As Lucia Reisch puts it,

> in order to save time, consumers buy new products instead of repairing them or reporting back to the store if they are broken, they limit information search to a sub-optimal extent, and they rely on invalid quality indicators such as brand names or price.
>
> (2001, p. 372)

Juliet Schor (1991, 1995) suggests a work and spend cycle sustained by institutional and economic conditions. Productivity gains are transformed into higher wages that are spent and consumers get used to higher levels of spending. The work and spend cycle implies locked-in properties of affluent life-styles where increased income primarily is used to raise consumption (Knight et al., 2013). Thus the proposed work and spend cycle, and consumer culture where product offerings are closely connected to identity and emotion, are seen as mutually reinforcing. Marketing practices such as advertising and branding, as well as the benefits of positioning consumption, become more effective when consumption per se is the main motivation for gaining higher income (Knight et al., 2013). In the same vein, Sullivan (2008) suggests temporal strategies of consumption used by the "work/consumption rich, time poor" framed by the idea that busyness, both in leisure and in employment, is one type of social differentiation and subsequent status distinction under the conditions of late capitalism (Gershuny,

2005). Sullivan suggests that "for higher socio-economic groups with money to spend, new avenues are created for establishing distinction and ensuring exclusion, and one of these avenues could be the establishment of multi-cultural capital through leisure participation" (2008, p. 14). Two such avenues, in terms of temporal strategies of consumption, are suggested that shed light on why higher income is paired with busyness and time famine, instead of increased leisure time. The first strategy implies frequent participation in a range of out-of-home leisure activities, e.g. classical ballet, sports events, eating out, sport participation, etc. Sullivan labels such high-paced and differentiated leisure activities "voracious" consumption (Sullivan and Katz-Gerro, 2007). Second, a temporal strategy of consumption is labelled inconspicuous consumption – the acquisition of expensive goods which are not used because there is no time (Sullivan and Gershuny, 2004).

Within recent sociology writings on affluent consumption and subsequent time shortages, the affluence-time relation is addressed as a matter of managing daily life in "a society in excess" (Löfgren and Czarniawska, 2012, p. 7). In Löfgren's and Czarniawska's books on the management of overflow of information, choices and consumption, consumers deal with overflow of goods through controlling and coping, using skills such as planning and multi-tasking (Löfgren and Czarniawska, 2012; Czarniawska and Löfgren, 2013). Their work on overflow as an organizational issue in the lives of affluent consumers contest a moralist critical stance vis-à-vis abundance attributed to Linder (1970), Lipovetsky (2006) and others. This book takes another position. It links abundant affluent consumption to environmental and social sustainable development which by default have moral dimensions. This book adheres to a view that can be summarized as "those who are questioning the wisdom of continuous economic growth are motivated by the fact that the planet has limited resources" (Knights et al., 2013, p. 692). By investigating the consequences of affluent consumption on sustainability and well-being, it is possible to describe the potential moral dimensions of such consumption without moralizing individual consumers' life-styles.

Sustainability outcomes of work rich, time poor affluent consumption

In addition to the general relationship between high incomes, high levels of consumption and emissions of greenhouse gases (Holmberg and Nässén, 2010) discussed in Chapter 1, there are specific work rich, time poor circumstances that add to our understanding of the general relationship between affluence and sustainability. When zooming in on how additional income is distributed among product categories, clear patterns emerge that partly explain why higher incomes entail higher emissions of CO_2. In Sweden, consumers spend additional income mostly on airborne holiday trips and on cars, whereas wealthy Americans spend less of their additional income on cars and more on larger residences (Holmberg and Nässén, 2010). One explanation for this difference in spending is time restriction: "it is not possible to travel much more due to scarcity of time, and instead one build climate-controlled mansions (to fill with all that stuff)" (Holmberg and Nässén, 2010, p. 229). Research on the impacts of time used working on emissions of greenhouse gases show that a decrease in work time of 1% reduces greenhouse gas emissions by 0.8% on average as a result of lower income and consumption (Nässén and Larsson, 2015). The impact of work time on the ecological footprint was investigated by Schor (2005), who found a positive correlation between the national ecological footprint and average hours per employee for 18 OECD-countries. In a similar study (on high income OECD countries) investigating the effect of work hours on the ecological footprint, the carbon footprint, and carbon dioxide emissions, it was found that time spent working is significantly associated with such environmental pressures (Knight et al., 2013). Such relationships are related to the so-called scale effect, which refers to more production and consumption enabled by greater income, and to the compositional effect, which implies that the greater the income, the more energy and material intensive consumption (see earlier discussion and Linder, 1970; Röpke, 2009).

Juliet Schor vividly describes the environmental effects of affluent consumption:

> it is important to remember that all manufactured goods have environmental effects associated with their production and in some cases, consumption. In many cases, these effects are substantial. Cotton production is pesticide intensive and depletes soil at a rapid rate . . . Textile and computer chip production are extremely water intensive. Leather tanning for shoes, handbags, clothing and other goods uses highly toxic substances and is contributing to significant water pollution in regions with tanning industries, such as South Asia. Computer production involves the intensive use of toxic metals, many of which are currently entering the waste stream (see Durning and Ryan, 1997). Mining for the precious metals that are used in jewelry and watches is extremely destructive to ecosystems. In addition, mining activities employ highly toxic chemicals. The ecological effects of automobile production and use have been widely documented. Toys, perhaps the least ecologically significant of the commodities discussed above, are nearly all plastic, and produced with toxic chemicals and with oil-intensive processes.

Ceteris paribus, increases in the consumption of all these products result in higher levels of toxic output, materials use, ecosystem degradation, and other negative environmental impacts.

(Schor, 2005, p. 215)

Time-related stressors

Structural time-related conditions that face Western affluent consumers who experience time scarcity (Glorieux et al., 2010; Sullivan, 2008) are related to dual-earner/dual-career households with highly qualified jobs, children and house ownership (Glorieux et al., 2010; Larsson, 2007; Sullivan, 2008). As mentioned earlier, work/income rich and time poor consumers apply various strategies to cope with the time pressures of ordinary life. As for leisure activities, perceived time shortages make very time-consuming activities less interesting, and practices that are materials-intensive and highly active become more popular (Röpke and Godskesen, 2007; Sullivan, 2008). The accounts of leisure (and work) busyness as a marker of status distinction in Western cultures of consumption form the basis for understanding affluent consumer time shortages as marketplace-induced stressors (Gershuny, 2005; Hochschild, 2005; Sullivan, 2008). From an embodied stress framework, time-related structural conditions – such as a lack of time for family and friends as well as existential consumption fuelled by perceived time shortages – are characteristic stressors of the work/income rich, time poor.

Stress caused by too little time with family

One chronic role strain connected to a work/income rich, time poor lifestyle is "too little time for family". Literature on the social consequences of working time (see review by Albertsen et al., 2008; Larsson, 2007) and work/life strategies (Moen and Yu, 2000) provides ample evidence

> that shorter work hours are used for activities such as child care, sleep, meals, social contacts, volunteer work (Albertsen et al., 2008) and these types of activities have also been shown to be more important for subjective well-being than material consumption acquired by increasing income (Layard, 2005).
>
> (Holmberg and Nässén, 2010, p. 232)

More leisure time and less working time, according to several studies, result in time spent taking care of children, cooking, upholding social contacts etc. Thus in line with an embodied stress understanding of consumption, time poverty among affluent consumers is connected to the chronic strains of an affluent life-style (Albertsen et al., 2008; Holmberg and Nässén, 2010; Layard, 2005). Moen and Yu (2000) show in their study on effective work/life strategies that when both spouses in US households work long hours (more than 45 hours per week), both men and the women experience high levels of stress, work/life conflict and overload. When working regular hours, they reported less stress. Recent literature suggests that the difficulties of combining work and family life have consequences already for young men and women in the affluent West (Koelet et al., 2015). Perceived multiple role pressures pile up early in life and cause delayed parenthood, among other things (Glorieux et al., 2010). The gender dimension of time pressure in work/income rich, time poor households is also emphasized in literature (Sullivan, 2008). Women are particularly vulnerable to time pressure, as mothers with young children and a career of their own have highly stressful schedules (Sullivan, 2008).

Affluent consumers apply various strategies to cope with time strains. Multi-tasking is

> a resolution of sorts to the pressures of time for those with restricted time for a multitude of tasks, and it has been shown to occur particularly among those with exceptionally full schedules such as dual-earner couples of young children and especially women within such households.
>
> (Sullivan, 2008, p. 8)

Thus multi-tasking is one dimension of the chronic role strain that face this group of consumers. Multi-tasking is a way to cope with time pressure (Löfgren, 2012) that most likely will increase the stress of an already time-pressed life-style (Mark et al., 2014; Wetherell and Carter, 2014). Stressful multi-tasking is explained as cognitive load and stress occurs when attentional thresholds are surpassed, cognitive capacities are overloaded and a loss of control is experienced (Jeong and Fishbein, 2007). In their study on the extent of ICT usage associated with stress in a sample of college students, Jeong and Fishbein (2007) show that ICT use "is an additional source of stress to other known stressors, e.g. academic performance or financial pressures" (p. 8). Multi-tasking stress is accompanied by increased heart rate and blood pressure (Wetherell and Carter, 2014). Multi-tasking is thus indicative of stress as "as taxing or exceeding his or her resources and endangering his or her wellbeing" (Lazarus and Folkman, 1984, p. 19) and, more specifically, of information and perceptual overload discussed in Chapter 4. In Chapter 4, information overload was described as "receiving too much information" and defined as occurring when information supply exceeds the limits of human information-processing capacities (Eppler and

Mengis, 2004; Jacoby et al., 1974; Scammon, 1977). We can conclude that multi-tasking, either as a way to cope with work/income rich, time poor life-style time pressures (Sullivan, 2008), or as a life-style characteristic of such life-styles (Löfgren, 2012), is understood as a chronic role strain from an embodied stress framework.

Existential consumption strains

In line with the "idealized identity" overload properties of Western consumer culture, it is highly probable that work/income rich, time poor consumers are particularly prone to experiencing internalized marketplace-induced chronic strains, as discussed in Chapter 5. This is because of their access to income available for consumption, but perhaps more importantly, because the affluent marketplace offers the possibility to consume in a compensatory manner. Compensatory consumption is undertaken mainly for existential reasons and provides quick answers to questions like "Who am I in relation to others?" The time constraints of work/income rich, time poor affluent consumers are assumed to favor such compensatory consumption. Conceptual studies suggest that material compensation of existential needs offers a solution to the anxieties of affluent consumers in the West (Reisch, 2001; Hochschild, 2005; Sullivan, 2008). Thus the condition of affluent consumers, characterized by rising income, increasing consumption and related feelings of time pressure, is closely connected to the meaning, or function, of consumption. Reisch (2001) argues that when we as (affluent) consumers repeatedly try to address our existential needs and questions with the positive emotions of consumption, the time-demanding human quality of reflection is inactive and forgotten.

The time pressure of affluent consumers is myopic in the sense that the literature reports that consumers do not know what to do with their time, and that shopping and consumption have become ways for people to spend time and find meaning in life (Csikszentmihalyi, 1999). This is in line with Schor's (1998) suggestion that in order for us to be able to consume less we must "fill the void"; shopping and other activities related to consuming goods and services fill that void in Western consumers' lives. The concept of compensation may provide one answer to the paradox of time pressure (Csikszentmihalyi, 1999). As affluent consumers, we experience time as plentiful when enacting and reproducing affluent consumption practices. In the sense that we "do our identity construction work" in the outside material world, not within ourselves, we spend relatively little time dwelling on the eternal questions of "who am I?" and "what am I doing with my life?" Indeed, consumption is a time-saving way of solving the existential puzzle, and time seems plentiful. The psychological risks connected to an acceleration of consumption were anticipated by Linder (1970) as time shortages would make it more difficult for us to engage in reflection that by default requires that demand patience and relaxation. Literature on affluent consumption and time spending support the claim that existential consumption, as consumption that compensates for reflection on meaning and identity, is at least partly linked to a work/income rich, time poor life-style. Hence, it seems that for affluent consumers, internalized marketplace-induced stressors are more severe.

The dispersed practice of work/income rich, time poor consumption

A useful concept in understanding work/income rich, time poor affluent consumption is the concept of dispersed practice. Schatzki (1996) distinguishes between dispersed and integrative practices. Dispersed practices (knowing how to) are general practices involved in many aspects of consumption, such as describing, explaining or imagining (Warde, 2005). Integrative practices are more specialized consumption practices constituting certain areas, such as cooking, gardening, parenting etc. Thus integrative practices include certain dispersed practices; for example, driving requires the component of imagining what happens if you don't have lights on your car. Warde (2005) argues that the performance of dispersed practices primarily "requires understanding" and "knowing how to do something, a capacity which presupposes a shared or collective practice involving performance in appropriate contexts and mastery of common understandings" (p. 135). The character of dispersed practices, as indicated by their widespread occurrence, makes them particularly relevant for the study of consumption. A specific dispersed practice follows from (1) the definition of affluent consumption in this book (Chapter 1) as *the financial possibility to consume in accordance with socially desirable consumption (fashion) trends* and (2) the recognition that affluent embodied consumption is shaped by the marketplace, in which idealized products and brands are heavily advertised. The dispersed practice of work/income rich, time poor affluent consumption (i.e. knowing how to consume as an affluent consumer) can be described as the process of self-assurance through purchase and use of consumption objects (products or services).

Affluent consumption in accordance with socially desirable consumption (fashion) trends is based on a shared understanding of consumption as a search for the socially acceptable and socially desirable. Affluent consumption practices that involve a relatively high degree of engagement, as in consumption of fashion or other conspicuous items or services, share traits with the existential function of Campbell's (2005) concept "craft consumption". In craft consumption, mass-produced products (e.g. fabrics and decorating materials) are used as raw material for the creation of a new product, such as a personalized style (of clothing or interior design). The suggested dispersed practice of work/income rich, time poor consumers – the process of self-assurance through purchase and use of consumption objects – has implications for the stress outcomes of work/income rich, time poor consumer life-styles. Consumption motivated by self-assurance compensates for time spent reflecting on meaning and identity. Environmental marketplace stressors experienced as perceptual overload is intimately connected to marketplace identity work characteristics of the work/income rich, time poor. In addition, internalized marketplace-induced stressors are more severe for consumers that partake in this kind of existential consumption to higher degrees (compared to consumers with less income and more time). Thus work/income rich, time poor affluent consumers face chronic role strains connected to the continuous supply of idealized and socially desirable product offerings in the affluent marketplace.

Bibliography

Albertsen, K., Rafnsdóttir, G.L., Grimsmo, A., Tomasson, K., and Kauppinen, K. (2008), Workhours and worklife balance. *Scandinavian Journal of Work, Environment & Health*, Vol. 34 No. 5, p. 14.

Campbell, C. (2005), The craft consumer culture, craft and consumption in a postmodern society. *Journal of Consumer Culture*, Vol. 5 No. 1, pp. 23–42.

Csikszentmihalyi, M. (1999), If we are so rich, why aren't we happy? *American Psychologist*, Vol. 54 No. 10, pp. 821–7.

Czarniawska, B., and Löfgren, O. (eds.). (2013), *Coping With Excess: How Organizations, Communities and Individuals Manage Overflows*, Edward Elgar Publishing, Cheltenham, UK.

Devetter, F., and Rousseau, S. (2011), Working hours and sustainable development. *Review of Social Economy*, Vol. 69 No. 3, pp. 333–55.

Eppler, M.J., and Mengis, J. (2004), The concept of information overload: A review of literature from organization science, accounting, marketing, MIS, and related disciplines. *Information Society*, Vol. 20 No. 5, pp. 325–44.

Gershuny, J. (2005), Busyness as the badge of honor for the new superordinate working class. *Social Research*, pp. 287–314.

Glorieux, I., Laurijssen, I., Minnen, J., and van Tienoven, T.P. (2010), In search of the harried leisure class in contemporary society: time-use surveys and patterns of leisure time consumption. *Journal of Consumer policy*, Vol. 33 No. 2, pp. 163–181.

Gronow, J., and Warde, A. (2001), *Ordinary Consumption* (Vol. 2), Psychology Press, New York.

Hochschild, A.R. (2005), On the edge of the time bind: Time and market culture. *Social Research: An International Quarterly*, Vol. 72 No. 2, pp. 339–54.

Holmberg, J., and Nässén, J. (2010), Well-being the path out of the consumption – Climate dilemma? *Beyond the Consumption Bubble*, Vol. 221.

Jacoby, J., Speller, D.E., and Kohn, C.A. (1974), Brand choice behavior as a function of information load. *Journal of Marketing Research*, Vol. 11 No. 1, pp. 63–9.

Jalas, M. (2002), A time use perspective on the materials intensity of consumption. *Ecological Economics*, Vol. 41 No. 1, pp. 109–123.

Jeong, S., and Fishbein, M. (2007), Predictors of multitasking with media: Media factors and audience factors. *Media Psychology*, Vol. 10 No. 3, pp. 364–84.

Knight, K.W., Rosa, E.A., and Schor, J.B. (2013), Could working less reduce pressures on the environment? A cross-national panel analysis of OECD countries, 1970–2007. *Global Environmental Change*, Vol. 23, pp. 691–700.

Koelet, S., Helga de Valk, A.G., Glorieux, I., Laurijssen, I., and Willaert, D. (2015), The timing of family commitments in the early work career: Work-family trajectories of young adults in Flanders. *Demographic Research*, Vol. 32, pp. 657–90.

Larsson, J. (2007), *Om föräldrars tidspress: orsaker och förändringsmöjligheter.* Research report 139, Gothenburg University, Sweden.

Layard, R. (2005), *Happiness: Lessons From a New Science*, Penguin, London.

Lazarus, R.S., and Folkman, S. (1984), *Stress, Appraisal, and Coping*, Springer Publishing Company, New York.

Linder, S.B. (1970), *The HARRIED leisure Class*, Columbia University Press, New York, p. 135.

Lipovetsky, G. (2006), *Le bonheur paradoxal: essai sur la société d'hyperconsommation* (Vol. 377). Gallimard, Paris.

Löfgren, O. (2012), It's simply too much! Coping with domestic overflow. *Managing Overflow in Affluent Societies*, pp. 101–24.

Löfgren, O., and Czarniawska, B. (2012), "The inherited theories of overflow and their challenges", in *Managing Overflows in Affluent Societies*, Routledge, New York, pp. 1–12.

Mark, G., Wang, Y., and Niiya, M. (2014, April), Stress and multitasking in everyday college life: an empirical study of online activity. In *Proceedings of the SIGCHI Conference on Human Factors in Computing Systems* (pp. 41–50). ACM.

Moen, P., and Yu, Y. (2000), Effective work/life strategies: Working couples, work conditions, gender, and life quality. *Social Problems*, Vol. 47, pp. 291–326.

Nässén, J., and Larsson, J. (2015), Would shorter working time reduce greenhouse gas emissions? An analysis of time use and consumption in Swedish households. *Environment and Planning C: Government and Policy*, Vol. 33 No. 4, pp. 726–45.

Reisch, L. (2001), Time and wealth: The role of time and temporalities for sustainable patterns of consumption. *Time and Society*, Vol. 10 No. 2, pp. 367–385.

Robinson, J., and Godbey, G. (1997), *Time for Life: The Surprising Ways that Americans Use their Time*, Pennsylvania State Press, Pennsylvania.

Ropke, I., and Godskesen, M. (2007), Leisure activities, time and environment. *International Journal of Innovation and Sustainable Development*, Vol. 2 No. 2, pp. 155–174.

Röpke, I. (2009), Theories of practice – New inspiration for ecological economic studies. *Ecological Economics*, Vol. 68, pp. 2490–7.

Sanne, C. (2002), Willing consumers – Or locked-in? Policies for a sustainable consumption. *Ecological Economics*, Vol. 42 No. 1, pp. 273–87.

Scammon, D.L. (1977), Information load and consumers. *Journal of Consumer Research*, Vol. 4 No. 3, pp. 148–55.

Schatzki, T. (1996), *Social Practices: A Wittgensteinian Approach to Human Activity and the Social*, Cambridge University Press, Cambridge.

Schor, J.B. (1991), *The Overworked American: The Unexpected Decline of Leisure*, Basic Books, New York.

Schor, J.B. (1995), "Can the north stop consumption growth? Escaping the cycle of work and spend", in Bhaskar, V., and Glyn, A. (eds.), *The North, the South and the Environment*, Earthscan, London.

Schor, J.B. (1998), *The Overspent American, Upscaling, Downshifting, and the New Consumer*, Basic Books, New York.

Schor, J.B. (2005), Sustainable consumption and worktime reduction. *Journal of Industrial Ecology*, Vol. 9 No. 1–2, pp. 37–50.

Southerton, D. (2003), Squeezing time' allocating practices, coordinating networks and scheduling society. *Time & Society*, Vol. 12 No. 1, pp. 5–25.

Sullivan, O. (2008), Busyness, status distinction and consumption strategies of the income rich, time poor. *Time & Society*, Vol. 17 No. 1, pp. 5–26.

Sullivan, O., and Gershuny, J. (2004), Inconspicuous consumption: Work-rich, time-poor in the liberal market economy. *Journal of Consumer Culture*, Vol. 4 No. 1, pp. 79–100.

Sullivan, O., and Katz-Gerro, T. (2007), The omnivore thesis revisited: Voracious cultural consumers. *European Sociological Review*, Vol. 23 No. 2, pp. 123–37.

Warde, A. (2005), Consumption and theories of practice. *Journal of Consumer Culture*, Vol. 5.

Wetherell, M.A., and Carter, K. (2014), The multitasking framework: The effects of increasing workload on acute psychobiological stress reactivity. *Stress and Health*, Vol. 30 No. 2, pp. 103–109.

Part 3

Stress coping and affluent sustainable consumption

7 Coping with marketplace stressors

As described in Chapter 3, coping in a consumption context is "the set of cognitive and behavioral processes initiated by consumers in response to emotionally arousing, stress inducing interactions with the environment aimed at bringing forth more desirable emotional states and reduced levels of stress" (Duhachek, 2005). This chapter describes how affluent consumers cope with marketplace-induced environmental, internalized and structural stressors, as described in Chapters 4, 5 and 6. Coping with marketplace-induced stress is, of course, difficult to separate from coping with work- or family-related stress. However, the focus in this chapter is on our coping as affluent consumers, not as parents or as employees.

Lazarus and Folkman (1984) propose that the body copes through efforts to restore balance following a stress-inducing disequilibrium as a result of threat or harm (Lazarus and Folkman, 1984; Moschis, 2007; Pearlin, 1983). Stress-coping strategies are categorized as active coping, through modifying the stressor (problem-focused strategies), and avoidance coping, which reduces the tension caused by the stressor (emotion-focused strategies) (Holahan and Moos, 1987; Lazarus and Folkman, 1984; Sapolsky, 2004; Thoits, 1995). Research on consumers' stress coping shows that support-seeking coping as an emotion-focused coping strategy dominates in the affluent marketplace (Duhachek, 2005). The construct of self-efficacy as the perception of one's own ability to cope with stress-related emotions explains why affluent consumers tend to seek social support when faced with marketplace stressors (Duhachek, 2005; Sujan et al., 1999). The reasons for why social support-seeking stress coping dominates in the affluent marketplace are described in Chapter 3. In short, the emotion of threat is most likely the dominant stress-related emotion in an affluent marketplace in which symbolic resources aimed at identity-making are paralleled with idealized and socially desirable products and services. Affluent consumers with access to financial resources to consume that which is regarded as socially desirable, as well as with access to social support structures, are regarded as self-efficient, i.e. they believe that adequate coping is within their reach (Sujan et al., 1999; Duhachek, 2005).

There is a lack of research that explicitly addresses consumers' stress coping in the context of chronic role strains. Literature that deals with consumption as a means to cope with stress following life events (Lee et al., 2001), daily hassles (Celuch and Showers, 1991) or meanings and emotions related to technological products (Mick and Fournier, 1998) provide interesting input for this book. However, coping with chronic affluent consumer role strains implies that coping strategies are intimately connected to affluent consumers' life-styles. In accordance with the embodied stress framework on which this book is built, stress coping is learned and afforded by the affluent marketplace (Dreyfus, 2002). As was discussed in Chapter 5, individualized and emotion-based identity-making expressed in consumption in affluent Western consumer culture(s) produces a continuous need for experiential input, which is provided in the affluent marketplace (Cherrier et al., 2012; Elliott, 2004; Jantzen et al., 2012; Mikkonen et al., 2014). Such commoditized identity-making has implications for marketplace-induced internalized stress but also, as this chapter highlights, for how inter-personal coping is undertaken as a response to consumer stress (Duhachek, 2005). Self-efficiency is an important concept here. Research suggests that self-efficient consumers, i.e. those who believe that adequate coping is within their reach, are more likely to use inter-personal coping strategies (Sujan et al., 1999). As will be discussed later, the affluent marketplace provides certain specific inter-personal coping strategies, namely socially accepted ways of knowing what to like and who to be. Thus, inasmuch as affluent consumption is a stress coping strategy in the consumer culture context, this way of coping with stress is dependent on social acceptance and social support. In the affluent marketplace, socially accepted stress coping is always within reach, provided by the fashion and advertising systems' offering of perpetual possibilities of self-formation, i.e. how to achieve an ideal self (Dittmar, 2008; Kasser, 2002; Miller, 2009).

Social support coping: gaining knowledge about how to consume in a socially acceptable manner

Consumers' social support stress coping – coping with marketplace-induced stress by consuming products and services that are socially acceptable and desirable – depends on available guidance and social support. One main tenet in this book is that affluent consumers use inter-personal strategies to cope with chronic role strains, and these strategies are afforded (provided and learned) by the affluent marketplace. Guidance and social support (coping strategies) provided in this marketplace are related to products' identity benefits and are communicated by expert systems such as advertising, brands, peers or aesthetic experts, which provide guidelines as to what to consume to alleviate stress connected to consumption choice and identity (Clarke and Miller, 2002; Warde, 1994; Turnbull et al., 2000; Woodward, 2006). Coping when faced with stress in terms of threats to cultural and social values connected to having the "wrong" products and taste, or not owing enough "cool" stuff, means to follow advice and guidance on what product offerings are desirable and "should" be purchased.

Clarke and Miller (2002) argue that for clothing most individuals do not know what their taste is and are too anxious to choose what clothing to buy without social (family and friends) or institutional support. In their study of female shopping of clothes in London, a shopping trip with Charmaigne, who has set out to buy a floral print is described:

> her mother and the researcher is a constant sounding board upon which to exchange opinions, with the sense that our approval might be seen as evidence against as for the garment in question. Even with all this support, the difficulty that was evident for Charmaigne, again and again, was knowing whether she actually liked a print or not and therefore being able to determine what her taste was or could be.
>
> (p. 197)

In their study they found that family relationships provide both support and ambivalence regarding choice of the "right outfit". Mail-order catalogues are used as a source of information that is "safe", objectively providing a consensus of what to wear in the office, in your leisure time, on Friday night etc. Self-assurance in the Western consumer culture context is likely to be dependent on buying products that provide meanings of idealized identity, continuously updated by fashion and media as novel products makes you the person you are expected to be, and hence you feel better (Elliott, 1994; Miller, 2001, 2009; Woodruffe-Burton and Elliott, 2005). Mikkonen et al. (2014) use the term "cultural intermediaries of the fashion system" to denote how consumers are dominated and manipulated:

> These intermediaries commonly include (1) the fashion designers that first propose new styles, (2) the "glossy magazines" and their editors and models that promote and showcase them in their respective media, and (3) the celebrities who wear them in paparazzi photographs. Glossy magazines such as Vogue, Harper's Bazaar, and Elle have an important role in the system, acting as "conduct manuals" to "feminine appearance" (Delhaye, 2006, p. 99). The editors of these magazines, such

as the infamous Anne Wintour, have been labelled as "the authorities" when it comes to clothing and accessories.

(Mikkonen et al., 2014, p. 257)

As already noted, coping as commoditized self-assurance shares many traits with Campbell's (2005) craft consumption. From the standpoint of the modern condition of moral differentiation, which is represented by individualized and commoditized identity-making taking place in the market, the craft consumer and the affluent consumer involved in stress coping seemingly represent the same kind of longing for self-assurance. In Western consumer cultures, "craft consumption could become highly valued because it is regarded as an oasis of personal self-expression and authenticity in what is an ever-widening 'desert' of commodification and marketization" (Campbell, 2005, p. 37).

Coping by compensatory consumption

The concept of compensatory consumption is helpful in understanding coping with chronic affluent marketplace-induced strains. The compensatory function of consumption is based on an understanding of consumption as reflecting either a correspondence between action and needs or, equally valid, a systematic *lack* of correspondence between action and needs (Gronmo, 1988; Grunert, 1993). Compensatory consumption "means that consumption is heavily emphasized as a reaction to, and as an attempt to make up for, a general lack of esteem or self-actualisation" (Gronmo, 1988, p. 68). Grunert (1993) defines compensatory consumption in the following way: "In general terms, the phenomenon is that a lack of x could be cured by a supply of x, but may also be cured by a supply of y. If y is used, this process is called compensation" (p. 76).

Building on the concept of compensatory consumption, the lack of stable and collective self-identity in Western consumer culture (discussed in Chapter 4) is compensated for by a supply of consumer goods associated with idealized/achieved identity images. Compensatory consumption includes different types of consumption undertaken for compensatory purposes (Woodruffe-Burton and Elliott, 2005) – such as compulsive buying (O'Guinn and Faber, 1989), self-gift giving (Mick and DeMoss, 1990) and addictive consumption (Elliott, 1994). The act of compensatory consumption is motivated by self-concept challenges, e.g. threats (Rucker and Galinsky, 2008; Shrum et al., 2014) to basic human needs of belonging, control, self-esteem and meaningfulness but also to culturally specified values, such as an exciting life or a beautiful body (Crocker and Knight,

2005; Gao et al., 2009). In short, literature on compensatory consumption suggests that material compensation of existential needs offers a solution to the anxieties of affluent consumers in the West (Reisch, 2001; Sullivan and Gershuny, 2004):

> People use goods not only to define their social status, but they become dependent on consumption because they substitute external goods for the fulfilment of inner needs: consumption is used as *compensation*. The more an individual uses consumption to satisfy inner needs and to fill an "empty self", the more importance he/she is likely to attach to the use of material goods as an indication of social standing.
>
> (Reisch, 2001, pp. 379–80)

Literature strongly suggests that compensatory consumption, whether in the form of shopping or buying food/beverages etc., could be seen a dimension of ordinary affluent consumption, i.e. not restricted to groups who might be considered to be vulnerable as compulsive buyers (Wood-ruffe, 1997). Following Gronmo's definition, a lack of stable self-identity in Western consumer culture causing a need for self-assurance and self-esteem could be cured by ascribed consumption related self-identities with subsequent self-assurance and self-esteem. Following this argument, litera-ture on compensatory consumption supports the argument in this book that the affluent marketplace, by supplying a constant flow of goods offering idealized/achieved identities, affords (provides) a normalized way for con-sumers to cope with stress connected to unstable identities. The compensa-tory function of consumption is central to my argument of a circuit of stress upholding sustainable levels of affluent consumption, which is discussed in Chapter 8.

Commoditized self-assurance and mood repair

One important function of objects consumed for compensatory reasons is insecurity alleviation, as they restore self-esteem and self-worth (Dit-tmar, 2005; Noguti and Bokeyar, 2014; Wicklund and Gollwitzer, 1981; Woodruffe-Burton and Elliott, 2005). In addition, psychological research provides evidence that the consumption of novel fashion goods plays a ther-apeutic role by making consumers feel better mood-wise (Dittmar, 2008; Luomala, 2002). From a stress theory perspective, compensatory consump-tion motivated by insecurity alleviation and mood repair is interpreted as an important support-seeking coping strategy learned in the affluent mar-ketplace (Carver and Scheier, 1994; Duhachek, 2005). According to stress theory, consumers with high self-esteem, strong social support and high socio-economic status are likely to be less affected by marketplace stressors (Moschis, 2007; Sapolsky, 2004; Thoits, 1995).

The mood-repairing and insecurity alleviating properties of consumption are described in material culture studies and psychological and consumer research (Clarke and Miller, 2002; Dittmar, 2008; Mick and DeMoss, 1990; Woodruffe-Burton and Elliott, 2005). Research evidence from numerous disciplines indicates that one specific type of affluent consumption, novelty shopping, takes on mood-repairing and self-assuring properties to ease negative psychological states and emotions related to anxiety and boredom (Burroughs and Rindfleish, 2002; Clarke and Miller, 2002; Dittmar, 2008; Mick and DeMoss, 1990; Moschis, 2007; O'Guinn and Faber, 1991; Pavia and Mason, 2004; Woodruffe-Burton and Elliott, 2005).

Mood-repairing shopping and shopping related to identity benefits are dimensions of self-gifts (Mick and DeMoss, 1990; Rook, 1987; Verplanken and Herabadi, 2001; Woodruffe-Burton and Elliott, 2005). Self-concept is an important dimension of self-gifts, including "self-definitional messages", such as when buying clothes after a difficult week to evoke feeling "like a new person" or buying antiques for the home to feel like a person who admires history (Mick and DeMoss, 1990). Luomala's (2002) phenomenological investigation about the therapeutic powers of mood-alleviating consumption among Finns provides evidence for a clear link between negative emotional states such as irritation, stress and dejection and consumption practice. The type of therapeutic power most clearly associated with stress-alleviating consumption activities was that of retreat, e.g. calming down or relaxing by reducing arousal (Luomala, 2002). Examples of mood-repairing shopping include retail therapy and compulsive buying, in which shopping is undertaken for mood management purposes (Atalay and Meloy, 2011; Elliott, 1994; Faber and Christenson, 1996; Faber and O'Guinn, 1989; Flight et al., 2012; Johnson and Attmann, 2009; Kacen, 1998; Kacen and Friese, 1999; Kang and Johnson, 2010; Müller et al., 2012; O'Guinn and Faber, 1991).

Psychologist Helga Dittmar's discussion of psychologically motivated shopping substantially informs our understanding of the relation between mood-repairing and insecurity alleviating affluent consumption. Shopping motivated by mood enhancement is "as much about wanting to feel better about oneself, as about simply wanting to feel better" (Dittmar, 2008, p. 103) because mood is interlinked with self-image and self-evaluation.

Research on mood-enhancing affluent consumption strongly suggests that buying motives among non-compulsory buyers are related to emotional and identity-related benefits as frequently as to functional motives (Dittmar,

2005, 2008). A four-week shopping diary study (including personal consumer goods and excluding routine household goods) with ordinary and compulsory buyers offers clear evidence for strong self-assuring motives of shopping for both groups, where the differences are only a matter of degree (Dittmar, 2005). These results provide evidence that affluent consumption is commonly motivated by mood-repair and insecurity alleviation. Affluent consumption can thus be considered as a type of compensatory consumption and stress coping, as it "means that consumption is heavily emphasized as a reaction to, and as an attempt to make up for, a general lack of esteem or self-actualisation" (Gronmo, 1988, p. 68).

Coping by consumption imagery

Literature proposes that coping with chronic role strains in the affluent marketplace – in particular structural stressors connected to the "work and consumption rich, time poor" affluent life-style – can take place in our imagination. Campbell's (1987, 1994) work on modern consumption related to imagery and daydreaming and Hochschild's concept of deferred use (2005) place coping in the imagined future. From this theoretical perspective affluent consumers' cope by thinking about their future experience of using consumption objects. Desire for future time is symbolized by purchases that provide an idealized identity – to be a good cook, a caring father etc. – once there is time to use the cooking gear and enjoy playing with the new toys together with the children. Inconspicuous consumption is closely related to Campbell's (1987) work on consumption as daydreaming where the purchase of an object is motivated by the imagination of its use. Access to time as a motivation for consumption is the materialization of deferred use (Hochschild, 2005). Consumption objects such as cooking gear, mountain bikes, toys etc. carry our hopes about future time spent with family or friends enjoying these objects. Imagined anticipated time spent using these objects makes "work and consumption rich, time poor" affluent consumers endure long working hours and time away from family and friends.

Affluent consumption: materialism or coping with marketplace-induced stress

The discussion of compensatory consumption as a way to cope with chronic role strains in the affluent marketplace implies that this marketplace is inherently stressful (otherwise stress coping would not be activated). The circle of stress and stress coping in the marketplace will be elaborated on in Chapter 8. However, before proceeding to this discussion we need to discuss materialist research in relation to the stress framework. Materialism, "a set of centrally held beliefs about the importance of possessions in one's life" (Richins and Dawson, 1992, p. 308), represents an individual value orientation that "indicates a conviction that material possessions can become sources of identity, to such an extent that they come to define who one is" (Dittmar, 2008a, p. 76). Psychological literature provides two main explanations for why materialism is associated with anxiety and hence indirectly with stress (Dittmar and Kapur, 2011; Kasser, 2002). First, materialism demands many hours of work and high levels of energy from individuals, implying less time and energy invested in activities that create happiness, such as spending time with family. Individuals who simultaneously are oriented towards material benefits and family values will be in a value conflict that is expected to lead to decreased well-being and psychological stress (Dittmar, 2008; Hobfoll, 1989). Second, materialism is related to personal/existential insecurity (Kasser, 2002; Rindfleisch et al., 2009), which is both a major cause of stress and a trigger for acquisition of consumption objects for stress coping purposes (Arndt et al., 2004; Maheswaran and Agrawal, 2004; Rindfleisch et al., 2009). The existential anxiety following the failure to satisfy inner needs is intimately connected to the time pressure following long working hours (Reisch, 2001; Sullivan, 2008). Stress caused by idealized products is triggered by materialistic ideals, mediated by the media, creating dissatisfaction with prior consumption choices (Kasser, 2002).

Affluent consumption conceptualized as stress coping challenges whether materialism is an individual value orientation (see Burroughs et al., 2013; Kasser, 2002; Rindfleisch et al., 2009). As discussed earlier, coping by means of novel fashion shopping indicates that consumer insecurities result from and are structural features of the fashion marketplace where new idealized products continuously are launched. Several consumer studies based on terror management theory, TNT, show that the probability that "materialistic preferences are heightened under conditions of existential insecurity" (Rindfleisch et al., 2009, p. 4) is empirically validated (Arndt et al., 2004; Maheswaran and Agrawal, 2004). In this book the absence of fixed identity anchors in Western consumer cultures create consumers who must define how to behave vis-à-vis others: they are free to decide on normativity, which is regarded as a major cause of stress (Clarke and Miller, 2002; Soron, 2010).

From a stress perspective, two types of insecurities that have been discussed in the materialism literature and identified by Rindfleisch et al. (2009) – personal and social – are caused by marketplace-induced strains. Thus the degree to which consumers are personally and socially insecure depends in part on how they cope with these marketplace-induced stressors. Personal insecurity (feelings of self-doubt; Troisi et al., 2006) and social insecurity (anxiety in social interactions) represent social and internalized strains, and the allostatic view on stress suggests that coping with such strains through consumption is a learned coping strategy. Materialism literature informs us that affluent consumers have no option but to cope with internalized and structural stressors integral to the affluent marketplace. The question thus remains how we as affluent consumers can, and should, cope given the sustainability outcomes of different coping strategies.

Bibliography

Arndt, J., Solomon, S., Kasser, T., and Sheldon, K. (2004), The urge to spurge: A terror management account of materialism and consumer behaviour. *Journal of Consumer Psychology*, Vol. 14 No. 3, pp. 198–212.

Atalay, A.S., and Meloy, M.G. (2011), Retail therapy: A strategic effort to improve mood. *Psychology & Marketing*, Vol. 28 No. 6, pp. 638–59.

Burroughs, J.E., Chaplin, L.N., Pandelaere, M., Norton, M.I., Ordabayeva, N., Gunz, A., and Dinauer, L. (2013), Using motivation theory to develop a transformative consumer research agenda for reducing materialism in society. *Journal of Public Policy & Marketing*, Vol. 32 No. 1, pp. 18–31.

Burroughs, J.E., and Rindfleish, A. (2002), Materialism and well-being: A conflicting values perspective. *Journal of Consumer Research*, Vol. 29, pp. 348–70.

Campbell, C. (1987), *The Romantic Ethic and the Spirit of Modern Consumerism*, Blackwell, London.

Campbell, C. (2005), The craft consumer culture, craft and consumption in a postmodern society. *Journal of Consumer Culture*, Vol. 5 No. 1, pp. 23–42.

Carver, C.S., and Scheier, M.F. (1994), Situational coping and coping dispositions in a stressful transaction. *Journal of Personality and Social Psychology*, Vol. 66 No. 1, p. 184.

Celuch, K., and Showers, L. (1991), It's time to stress stress: The stress-purchase/ consumption relationship: Suggestions for research. *Advances in Consumer Research*, Vol. 18, pp. 284–9.

Cherrier, H., Szuba, M., and Özcaglar-Toulouse, N. (2012), Barriers to downward carbon emission: Exploring sustainable consumption in face of the glass floor. *Journal of Marketing Management*, Vol. 28 No. 3–4, pp. 397–419.

Clarke, A., and Miller, D. (2002), Fashion and anxiety. *Fashion Theory*, Vol. 6 No. 2, pp. 191–214.

Crocker, J., and Knight, K.M. (2005), Contingencies of self-worth. *Current Directions in Psychological Science*, Vol. 14 No. 4, pp. 200–3.

Delhaye, C. (2006), The development of consumption culture and the individualization of female identity: Fashion discourse in the Netherlands 1880–1920. *Journal of Consumer Culture*, Vol. 6 No. 1, pp. 87–115.

Dittmar, H. (2005), A new look at 'compulsive buying': Self-discrepancies and materialistic values as predictors of compulsive buying tendency. *Journal of Social and Clinical Psychology*, Vol. 24, pp. 806–33.

Dittmar, H. (2008), *Consumer Culture, Identity and Well-Being*, Psychology Press, New York.

Dittmar, H., and Kapur, P. (2011), Consumerism and well-being in India and the UK: Identity projection and emotion regulation as underlying psychological processes. *Psychology Studies*, Vol. 56 No. 1, pp. 71–85.

Dreyfus, H.L. (2002), Intelligence without representation – Merleau-Ponty's critique of mental representation the relevance of phenomenology to scientific explanation. *Phenomenology and the Cognitive Sciences*, Vol. 1 No. 4, pp. 367–83.

Duhachek, A. (2005), Coping: A multidimensional, hierarchical framework of responses to stressful consumption episodes. *Journal of Consumer Research*, Vol. 32 No. 1, pp. 41–53.

Elliott, R. (1994), Addictive consumption: Function and fragmentation in postmodernity. *Journal of Consumer Policy*, Vol. 17 No. 2, pp. 159–79.

Elliott, R. (2004), "Making up people: Consumption as a symbolic vocabulary for the construction of identity", in Ekström, K., and Brembeck, H. (eds.), *Elusive Consumption*, Berg Publishers, Oxford, pp. 11–25.

Faber, R.J., and Christenson, G.A. (1996), In the mood to buy: Differences in the mood states experienced by compulsive buyers and other consumers. *Psychology & Marketing*, Vol. 13 No. 8, pp. 803–19.

Faber, R.J., and O'Guinn, T.C. (1989), Classifying compulsive consumers: Advances in the development of a diagnostic tool. *NA-Advances in Consumer Research*, Vol. 16.

Flight, R.L., Rountree, M.M., and Beatty, S.E. (2012), Feeling the urge: Affect in impulsive and compulsive buying. *Journal of Marketing Theory and Practice*, Vol. 20 No. 4, pp. 453–66.

Gao, L., Wheeler, S.C., and Shiv, B. (2009), The 'shaken self': Product choices as a means of restoring self-view confidence. *Journal of Consumer Research*, Vol. 36 No. 1, pp. 29–38.

Gronmo, S. (1988), "Compensatory consumer behaviour: Elements of a critical sociology of consumption", in Otnes, P. (ed.), *The Sociology of Consumption*, Solum Forlag, Norway and Humanities Press, New York.

Grunert, S.C. (1993), "On gender differences in eating behaviour as compensatory consumption", in Costa, A. (ed.), *Proceedings of the Second Conference on Gender and Consumer Behaviour*, University of Utah, Salt Lake City, UT, pp. 74–86.

Hobfoll, S.E. (1989), Conservation of resources: A new attempt at conceptualizing stress. *American Psychologist*, Vol. 44 No. 3, p. 513.

Hochschild, A.R. (2005), On the edge of the time bind: Time and market culture. *Social Research: An International Quarterly*, Vol. 72 No. 2, pp. 339–54.

Holahan, C.J., and Moos, R.H. (1987), Personal and contextual determinants of coping strategies. *Journal of Personality and Social Psychology*, Vol. 52 No. 5, pp. 946–55.

Jantzen, C., Fichett, J., Ostergaard, P., and Vetner, M. (2012), Just for fun? The emotional regime of experiential consumption. *Marketing Theory*, Vol. 12 No. 2, pp. 137–54.

Johnson, T., and Attmann, J. (2009), Compulsive buying in a product specific context: Clothing. *Journal of Fashion Marketing and Management: An International Journal*, Vol. 13 No. 3, pp. 394–405.

Kacen, J.J. (1998), Retail therapy: Consumers' shopping cures for negative moods. *Advances in Consumer Research*, Vol. 25 No. 1, pp. 75–87.

Kacen, J.J., and Friese, S. (1999), An exploration of mood-regulating consumer buying behavior. *European Advances in Consumer Research*, Vol. 4, pp. 73–6.

Kang, M., and Johnson, K.K. (2010), Let's shop! Exploring the experiences of therapy shoppers. *Journal of Global Fashion Marketing*, Vol. 1 No. 2, pp. 71–9.

Kasser, T. (2002), *The High Price of Materialism*, The MIT Press, Cambridge, MA.

Lazarus, R.S., and Folkman, S. (1984), *Stress, Appraisal, and Coping*, Springer Publishing Company, New York.

Lee, E., Moschis, G., and Mathur, A. (2001), A study on life events and changes in patronage preferences. *Journal of Business Research*, Vol. 54, pp. 25–38.

Luomala, H.T. (2002), An empirical analysis of the practices and therapeutic power of mood-alleviative consumption in Finland. *Psychology & Marketing*, Vol. 19 No. 10, pp. 813–36.

Maheswaran, D., and Agrawal, N. (2004), Motivational and cultural variations in mortality salience effects: Contemplations on terror management theory and consumer behavior. *Journal of Consumer Psychology*, Vol. 14 No. 3, pp. 213–18.

Mick, D.G., and DeMoss, M. (1990), Self-gifts: Phenomenological insights from four contexts. *Journal of Consumer Research*, pp. 322–32.

Mick, D.G., and Fournier, S. (1998), Paradoxes of technology: Consumer cognizance, emotions and coping strategies. *Journal of Consumer Research*, Vol. 25, pp. 123–43.

Mikkonen, I., Vicdan, H., and Markkula, A. (2014), What not to wear? Oppositional ideology, fashion, and governmentality in wardrobe self-help. *Consumption Markets & Culture*, Vol. 17 No. 3, pp. 254–73.

Miller, D. (2001), "Behind closed doors", in Miller, D. (ed.), *Home Possessions*, Berg, Oxford pp. 1–23.

Miller, D. (2009), "Buying time", in Shove, E., Trentmann, F., and Wilk, R. (eds.), *Time, Consumption and Everyday Life: Practice, Materiality and Culture*, Berg, Oxford, pp. 157–70.

Moschis, G.P. (2007), Stress and consumer behavior. *Journal of the Academy of Marketing Science*, Vol. 35 No. 3, pp. 430–44.

Müller, A., Mitchell, J.E., Crosby, R.D., Cao, L., Johnson, J., Claes, L., and de Zwaan, M. (2012), Mood states preceding and following compulsive buying episodes: An ecological momentary assessment study. *Psychiatry Research*, Vol. 200 No. 2, pp. 575–80.

Noguti, V., and Bokeyar, A.L. (2014), Who am I? The relationship between self-concept uncertainty and materialism. *International Journal of Psychology: Journal International de Psychologie*, Vol. 49 No. 5, pp. 323–33.

O'Guinn, T.C., and Faber, R.J. (1989), Compulsive buying: A phenomenological exploration. *Journal of Consumer Research*, Vol. 16 No. 2, pp. 147–57.

O'Guinn, T.C., and Faber, R.J. (1991), Mass communication and consumer behavior. *Handbook of Consumer Behavior*, Vol. 349, p. 400.

Pavia, T.M., and Mason, M.J. (2004), The reflexive relationship between consumer behaviour and adaptive coping. *Journal of Consumer Research*, Vol. 3, pp. 441–54.

Pearlin, L. (1983), "Role strains and personal stress", in Kaplan, H.B. (ed.), *Psychosocial Stress: Trends in Theory and Research*, Academic Press, New York, pp. 3–30.

90   *Stress coping and consumption*

Reisch, L. (2001), Time and wealth: The role of time and temporalities for sustainable patterns of consumption. *Time and Society*, Vol. 10 No. 2, pp. 367–385.

Richins, M.L., and Dawson, S. (1992), Materialism as a consumer value: Measure development and validation. *Journal of Consumer Research*, Vol. 19, pp. 303–16.

Rindfleisch, A., Burroughs, J.E., and Wong, N. (2009), The safety of objects: Materialism, existential insecurity, and brand connection. *Journal of Consumer Research*, Vol. 36 No. 1, pp. 1–16.

Rook, D.W. (1987), The buying impulse. *The Journal of Consumer Research*, Vol. 14 No. 2, pp. 189–99.

Rucker, D.D., and Galinsky, A.D. (2008), Desire to acquire: Powerlessness and compensatory consumption. *Journal of Consumer Research*, Vol. 35 No. 2, pp. 257–67.

Sapolsky, R.M. (2004), *Why Zebras Don't Get Ulcers: The Acclaimed Guide to Stress, Stress-Related Diseases, and Coping – Now Revised and Updated*, Macmillan, New York.

Shrum, L.J., Lowrey, T.M., Pandelaere, M., Ruvio, A.A., Gentina, E., Furchheim, P., . . . and Steinfield, L. (2014), Materialism: The good, the bad, and the ugly. *Journal of Marketing Management*, Vol. 30 No. 17–18, pp. 1858–81.

Soron, D. (2010), Sustainability, self-identity and the sociology of consumption. *Sustainable Development*, Vol. 18, pp. 172–81.

Sujan, M., Sujan, H., Bettman, J., and Verhallen, T. (1999), "Sources of consumers' stress and their Coping Strategies", in Dubois, B., Lowrey, T., and Shrum, L. (eds.), *European Advances in Consumer Research* (Vol. 4), Association for Consumer Research, Provo, UT, pp. 182–7.

Sullivan, O. (2008), Busyness, status distinction and consumption strategies of the income rich, time poor. *Time and Society*, Vol. 17, pp. 5–26.

Sullivan, O., and Gershuny, J. (2004), Inconspicuous consumption: Work-rich, time-poor in the liberal market economy. *Journal of Consumer Culture*, Vol. 4 No. 1, pp. 79–100.

Thoits, P. (1995), Stress, coping and social support processes: Where are we? What next? *Journal of Health and Social Behaviour*, Vol. 35, pp. 53–79.

Troisi, J.D., Christopher, A.N., and Marek, P. (2006), Materialism and money spending disposition as predictors of economic and personality variables. *North American Journal of Psychology*, Vol. 8 No. 3.

Turnbull, P.W., Leek, S., and Ying, G. (2000), Customer confusion: The mobile phone market. *Journal of Marketing Management*, Vol. 16 No. 1–3, pp. 143–63.

Verplanken, B., and Herabadi, A. (2001), Individual differences in impulse buying tendency: Feeling and no thinking. *European Journal of Personality*, Vol. 15 No. S1, pp. S71–S83.

Warde, A. (1994), Consumption, identity-formation and uncertainty. *Sociology*, Vol. 28 No. 4, pp. 877–98.

Warde, A. (2005), Consumption and theories of practice. *Journal of Consumer Culture*, Vol. 5.

Wicklund, R.A., and Gollwitzer, P.M. (1981), Symbolic self-completion, attempted influence, and self-deprecation. *Basic and Applied Social Psychology*, Vol. 2 No. 2, pp. 89–114.

Woodruffe-Burton, H.R. (1997), Compensatory consumption (or: Why do women go shopping when they're fed up? And other stories). *Marketing Intelligence and Planning*, Vol. 15 No. 7, pp. 325–34.

Woodruffe-Burton, H.R., and Elliott, R. (2005), Compensatory consumption and narrative identity theory. *Advances in Consumer Research*, Vol. 32, p. 461.

Woodward, I. (2006), Investigating consumption anxiety thesis: Aesthetic choice, narrativisation and social performance. *The Sociological Review*, Vol. 54 No. 2, pp. 263–82.

8 Consumer coping strategies and sustainable consumption outcomes

This chapter focuses on the relation between affluent consumers' stress coping and sustainable consumption. By discussing consumers' available stress coping options, an answer to Campbell's question – "The problem to be addressed when attempting to account for modern consumption, therefore, is how it is possible for inexhaustible wants, often wants for novel products and services – to appear with such regularity" (1994, p. 515) – can be proposed. One of the rationales for applying a stress perspective to the study of affluent sustainable consumption is the potential of such a framework to guide coping strategies that reduce affluent consumption. The embodied stress circuit of stress presented in Chapter 3 – where affluent marketplace stressors sustain affluent consumption through social support-seeking coping – is in this chapter illustrated as a spiral (see Figure 8.1). This spiral is designed to make clear the important message in this book: that marketplace-induced stressors and marketplace-afforded coping strategies fuel affluent consumption. However, stress theory stipulates that alternative stress coping strategies might have the opposite effect; affluent consumption would probably be reduced if alternatives to inter-personal coping were provided (by various societal actors) and applied by consumers – such a scenario is illustrated in Figure 8.2.

The enforcing relationship between marketplace stressors, body reactions and support-seeking coping as consumption that was explored in Chapters 4 through 7 delineates the contours of a vicious spiral of chronic affluent consumer stressors primarily coped with by consumption. The self-sustaining and stress-informed spiral of affluent consumption in Figure 8.1 offers an embodied explanation to the seemingly ever-increasing affluent consumption that follows disposable income (see Chapter 1). The sustainability consequences of such a spiral are very problematic, as ever-increasing affluent consumption requires large inputs of resources and energy.

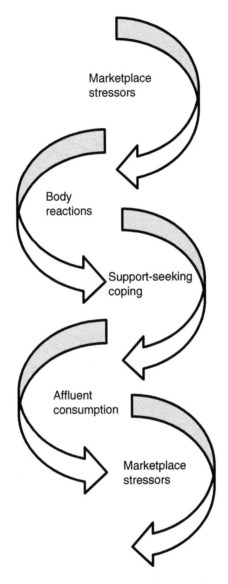

Figure 8.1 Marketplace-induced stressors and marketplace-afforded support-seeking coping strategies fuel continuous affluent consumption

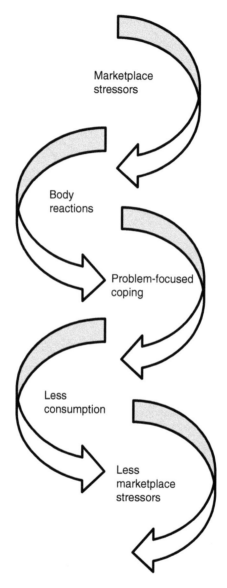

Figure 8.2 Marketplace-induced stressors and problem-focused coping reduce affluent consumption

Similar to the stress-informed spiral of affluent consumption in Figure 8.1, vicious cycles of insecurity and consumption are described in materialism studies. The proposed stress-consumption spiral shares many traits with Kasser's (2002) description of a vicious circle in which consumer culture ideals and subsequent materialistic values lead to chronic experiences of discrepancies and dissatisfaction. Short-term, alluring, self-bolstering effects of compensatory consumption that decrease well-being in the long run (see Shrum et al., 2014 for a review) form the basis for materialist research disputing the long-term effects of materialistic behaviours – including shopping – on insecurity alleviation (Burroughs and Rindfleisch, 2002; Kasser, 2002; Noguti and Bokeyar, 2014; Shrum et al., 2014; Wang and Wallendorf, 2006). Recent materialism literature accordingly proposes that initiatives that aim to reduce affluent consumption must focus on building consumer self-confidence to reduce the inclination to buy new products to alleviate insecurities (Burroughs et al., 2013). Such self-confidence coping (just like support-seeking coping) is emotion-focused coping and aims to reduce the tension of the social and internal (internalized) strains that consumption relieves. The basic premise of reducing materialism, as enacted in affluent consumption through building self-esteem, is that "if people feel good about themselves, they should feel less inclined to rely on external objects for reassurance and validation" (Burroughs et al., 2013, p. 22). Consequently, Burroughs et al. argue that experiential consumption, prosocial giving and the development of self-esteem in children might lead to strengthened personal and social welfare, which build self-confidence and result in less materialism. The stress perspective presented in this book rests on allostatic assumptions, which imply that the body (including the mind) assesses stressors and automatically seeks to restore balance when faced with stressors that threaten bodily equilibrium. In this book an abundance of evidence has been presented on affluent consumer role strains and coping strategies provided (afforded) by the affluent marketplace through marketing practice. In such a marketplace potential effectiveness of self-confidence building as an emotion-focused coping strategy for purposes of reducing affluent consumption is challenged. From an allostatic stress perspective, affluent consumers will more or less automatically react to marketplace-induced stressors as an embodied attempt to restore bodily balance and control. From this line of reasoning it follows that increased consumer self-confidence will stand little chance as a strategy to reduce affluent consumption. Instead, the stress theory framework provides arguments for active coping strategies which are oriented toward modifying the stressors, or so-called problem-focused coping strategies (Holahan and Moos, 1987; Lazarus and Folkman, 1984; Sapolsky, 2004; Thoits,

1995). Problem-focused coping implies actively managing marketplace-induced stressors through actions such as changing consumption behavior, e.g. refraining from engaging in shopping and related activities, such as browsing around stores, reading fashion magazines and blogs etc. (Duhachek, 2005; Moschis, 2007). Problem-focused coping also includes seeking information about alternative ways to spend money otherwise spent on consumption of good and services (Duhachek, 2005; Moschis, 2007). Figure 8.2 illustrates the reducing effect of problem-focused coping on affluent consumption.

According to the embodied stress theory framework, problem-focused coping applied to affluent marketplace-induced stressors – such as less time and engagement spent browsing e-shops or window shopping or using fashion media, and more time and attention directed at other types of less stressful activities – would lessen the effect of marketplace stressors on consumers and subsequently on affluent consumption. Chronic affluent consumer role strains, for example the perceptual and idealized identity overload related to the continuous supply of novel objects in industries of fashion, will decrease if there is a decline in the time and attention shoppers spend looking for novel fashion objects. Consumers' experiences of threat-related emotions or thought content linked to previous versions of fashion objects – which follow from launches of new fashion objects in accordance with the stress theory framework – will decline if less attention is paid to new product launches. The sustainability gains of problem-focused coping, as illustrated in Figure 8.2, is less affluent consumption (and consequently less use of energy and resources for the production of goods and services) which leads to less chronic marketplace-induced stress; this in turn will be coped with using problem-focused coping, leading to less consumption etc.

Can problem-focused coping be promoted?

How can problem-focused coping be promoted and facilitated as a stress coping strategy in the affluent marketplace? Without any doubt, problem-focused coping challenges marketplace actors, including consumers, businesses and policymakers, to engage in reducing affluent consumption for reasons of sustainability and consumer well-being. Theoretically, problem-focused stress coping is challenged by everyday consumer practices described in sustainable consumption literature. Discursive understandings of sustainable consumption assume that consumers need help minimizing the confusion arising from seemingly contradictory ways of consuming sustainably and that minimizing this confusion will reduce the affluent consumption (Markkula and Moisander, 2012; Moisander et al., 2010). Whereas consumers' discursive confusion is supposed to be alleviated by providing them with coherent sustainable consumption meanings, including active political responsibility (Markkula and Moisander, 2012), problem-focused stress coping includes avenues to reduce affluent consumption by various measures that circumscribe access to novel consumption objects and their representations. Higher priced consumption objects that slow down the pace of replacing existing objects with new ones, and higher priced fashion media that affect the inclination to buy novel fashion objects for reasons of social desirability, are examples of measures that indirectly affect access to consumption objects.

More politically correct measures in line with problem-focused coping that aims to reduce affluent consumption is the strengthening of non-consumption sources of intense emotional experiences in social life (Rafferty, 2011). Such measures are in line with the current regime of individual freedom, in which desirable experiential input forms the basis of identity (Campbell, 2004; Denegri-Knott and Molesworth, 2010; Elliott, 1997, 2004; Jantzen et al., 2012; Shankar et al., 2006). Any experience that provides desirable emotions might replace consumption as ontological reassurance (Campbell, 2004). Thus, initiatives promoting non-material sources of consumers' emotional experience might help decrease the environmentally adverse effects of continuous affluent consumption and chronic consumer role strains produced by the affluent marketplace.

Marketing governmentality and problem-focused stress coping

As described earlier, problem-focused stress coping means 1) less time and engagement spent in the affluent marketplace and 2) replacing consumption-related intense emotional experience with non-consumption sources of desired emotions. In many ways, problem-focused stress coping stands in sharp contrast to contemporary marketing practice. Marketing research strongly suggests that consumers' perceptions of value and choice of products is dependent on marketing practices such as branding and advertising, both in terms of content and frequency (Erdem et al., 2008; Grewal et al., 1998; Zeithaml, 1988). Branding and advertising are examples of marketing practices that produce norms by suggesting desired life-styles compatible with specific brands, hence shaping the sustainability of consumption (Arvidsson, 2005; Caruana and Crane, 2008; Zwick et al., 2008). Marketing practices thus can be regarded as highly influential in shaping carbon life-styles (Southerton et al., 2004).

Governing the consumer, and thus consumers' choice of products through desire, is regarded as a process of self-governmentality, imposed by messages (conveyed primarily by advertising) encouraging the individual to improve his/her life, body, home or wardrobe by consuming specific products or experiences. This process of governing the consumer subject as a sovereign self-entrepreneur (Beckett, 2012; Moisander et al., 2010; Zwick and Cayla, 2011) constructs consumer freedom as a means of control (Shankar et al., 2006; Zwick et al., 2008). Examples from Sweden – the context in which this book has been written and a country representing an affluent marketplace within Western consumer culture – illustrate the material and discursive construction of consumption produced by marketing practice (Caruana and Crane, 2008; Cova and Cova, 2012; Markkula and Moisander, 2012). In the Swedish affluent marketplace, exotic holiday destinations, recreation activities such as gardening, home decoration and indoor renovation (the two latter are positioned as the ultimate recreation for happy people in advertising for DIY-retailers) are communicated as idealized and fashionable life-style options frequently described in magazines and TV programmes. Supply and availability of branded goods is a prerequisite for business to market these activities as part of an ideal identity. The intimate connection between a rich supply of fashionable/trendy products and marketing discourse idealization is illustrated by the development of the Swedish market for home decoration. Fuentes describes the expansion of the home decoration market in the period 1990–2006. During this time, established retailers expanded and new retailers entered the market (Fuentes, 2011). Sales figures skyrocketed 2005–2006 and there was a parallel explosive increase in the number of Swedish home decoration magazines, and a number of home decoration TV programs were launched. Home decoration consumption was constructed as idealized identity-making.

Marketing governs consumers in different ways. Moisander et al. (2010) suggest four interrelated dimensions of marketing governance that are relevant for our understanding of sustainable consumption. (1) Visibilities and visual representation, which include images in advertising and in-store visual spatial arrangements such as lighting, colour and materials designed to construct specific shopping experiences. (2) Knowledge and expertise to define the consumer. Through technologies of consumption such as loyalty club programmes or other forms of marketing intelligence, marketers use detailed consumer knowledge to construct and suggest ways of being (identity positions) that necessitate specific products and brands (Beckett, 2012). (3) Techniques and practices of government such as segmentation and product development build on know-how about consumers acquired through market intelligence. Product development, in terms of product replacement, is used by the fashion industry as well as providers of domestic appliances. Seasonal trends and frequent style modifications through the launches of new collections, types or colours create consumer desire to constantly update their arsenal of products. (4) Identities and forms of identification build on both the visual imaginary in marketing and the knowledge about consumers provided by marketing intelligence and new product launches. In the fast fashion industry, marketing discourse-based identity idealization via visual imagery in advertising is coupled with frequent launches of new collections and styles (Joy et al., 2012; Schroeder and Zwick, 2004). Fast fashion provides cheap chic and fast cycles of fashion, often based on limited editions offering idealized personalization of the mass-customized (Joy et al., 2012). In sum these governmentality techniques have severe environmental consequences given the heavy use of water and pesticides in cotton farming. The same interconnection between identity idealization in advertising and ample product supply is found in the markets for new recreational experiences (challenging sports that will shape the body and exciting adventures that challenge the mind) and exotic holiday destinations, or combinations of the two (going to Thailand to learn yoga), which spur affluent consumption of recreation experiences and air travel. Consumption of recreation and travel corresponds to an expanding tourism and leisure industry that has grown by 1–2% per year for the last 30 years and where advertising, connecting (exotic) destinations and leisure activities to ideal life style aspirations, is booming (Morgan et al., 2012).

Marketing governmentality is not a disciplining technique but a construction of consumers' free will to internalize a problematization of the self and to achieve self-improvement goals that are in the interest of the marketer, which is the essence of the concept self-governmentality (Rose, 1999). The identity position of the self-governed consumer stands in sharp contrast to problem-focused stress coping. Permanent self-improvement through consumption choice as the key identity position provided by marketing practice, holds back collective norms and stable identity positions (Zwick and Cayla, 2011). Without such norms and identity positions, marketing discourse inevitably ends up constructing affluent consumption without questioning the level of consumption, even though efforts are made to make affluent consumption more sustainable through the use of green imagery, low GHG intense products and sustainable values (Caruana and Crane, 2008; Kadirov and Varey, 2013). As a result, marketing practice that sustains consumer identities of constant self-improvement through commodity choice will risk contributing to environmentally and socially harmful production and consumption practices (as the volume of goods produced/consumed remain unquestioned).

It seems improbable that affluent sustainable consumption can be promoted within the same commodity discourse that fuels ever-increasing levels of consumption (Dobers and Strannegård, 2005). The main tenet of using existing commodity discourse to promote sustainable consumption is market actors' ability to change the manner of speaking about consumption objects and include environmental degradation and social injustice in commoditized identity meanings (Prothero and Fitchett, 2000; Prothero et al., 2010; Soper, 2007). Within the academic community there are diverging views on if and how commoditized identity-making effectively can contribute to sustainable consumption (Dolan, 2002; Prothero et al., 2010). Some researchers suggest that marketing practice as described above is incompatible with consumption for the sake of the common good, as (marketing) tools and techniques produce a culture of self-government (Zwick and Cayla, 2011). Empirical studies contest efforts to promote sustainability through existing consumer cultures of differentiation and self-governmentality.

> Although *technological improvements* no doubt have great potential to reduce the environmental impacts of current lifestyles, their contribution to sustainable consumption still *has limits*. Despite the impressive results in process and product efficiency and the increasing share of eco-labelled products on the market, the aggregate levels of emissions from product consumption are increasing, the amount of products per household and per person is growing and the overall size and speed of resource and waste flows in society are mounting.
>
> (Mont et al., 2013, p. 26)

Sustainable products may be more energy efficient per unit, but this resource gain is outweighed if products are getting larger, such as TVs and car engines, or smaller, such as electronic products in which the production of small-size units requires high levels of energy use, toxic compounds and scarce materials such as "rare metals" (Mont et al., 2013). Recent data clearly shows how the fuel efficiency of cars has improved over recent decades, while these energy gains have been offset by an increase in European car travel (EEA, 2012). As a result, the fuel efficiency of cars have enabled people to drive longer distances without spending more money, indicating intriguing relationships between disposable income and private consumption. Rebound effects are commonplace in the household context. Money saved from installing energy saving devices in the home or from selling a second car is potentially spent on high climate impact products and services, such as flying on holiday (Brännlund et al., 2007; Platt and Retallack, 2009).

As stated in Chapter 1, the rationale for discussing affluent consumption from a stress perspective is the potential of problem-focused coping strategies to reduce affluent consumers' stress and unsustainable consumption. However, the affluent consumer and marketplace practices discussed earlier, in particular dominant marketing governmentality techniques, offer a rather dark picture regarding the possibilities of problem-focused coping to be provided (afforded) by contemporary affluent marketplaces. In essence, problem-focused coping in the affluent marketplace (spending less time, attention and money in this marketplace) stand in sharp contrast to constant self-improvement through consumption. In Chapter 10, possible solutions to the contradictory positions of problem-focused coping and marketing practices in affluent marketplaces will be explored.

Bibliography

Arvidsson, A. (2005), Brands: A critical perspective. *Journal of Consumer Culture*, Vol. 5 No. 2, pp. 235–58.

Beckett, A. (2012), Governing the consumer: Technologies of consumption. *Consumption Markets & Culture*, Vol. 15 No. 1, pp. 1–18.

Brännlund, R., Ghalwash, T., and Nordström, J. (2007), Increased energy efficiency and the rebound effect: Effects on consumption and emissions. *Energy Economics*, Vol. 29 No. 1, pp. 1–17.

Burroughs, J.E., Chaplin, L.N., Pandelaere, M., Norton, M.I., Ordabayeva, N., Gunz, A., and Dinauer, L. (2013), Using motivation theory to develop a transformative consumer research agenda for reducing materialism in society. *Journal of Public Policy & Marketing*, Vol. 32 No. 1, pp. 18–31.

Burroughs, J.E., and Rindfleisch, A. (2002), Materialism and well-being: A conflicting values perspective. *Journal of Consumer Research*, Vol. 29 No. 3, pp. 348–70.

Campbell, C. (1994), Consuming goods and the good of consuming. *Critical Review*, Vol. 8 No. 4, pp. 503–20.

Campbell, C. (2004), "I shop therefore I know that I am: The metaphysical basis of modern consumerism", in Ekström, K. and Brembeck, H. (eds.), *Elusive Consumption*, Berg Publishers, Oxford, pp. 27–44.

Caruana, R., and Crane, A. (2008), Constructing consumer responsibility: Exploring the role of corporate communications. *Organization Studies*, Vol. 29 No. 12, pp. 1495–519.

Cova, B., and Cova, V. (2012), On the road to prosumption: Marketing discourse and the development of consumer competencies. *Consumption Markets & Culture*, Vol. 15 No. 2, pp. 149–68.

Denegri-Knott, J., and Molesworth, M. (2010), 'Love it. Buy it. Sell it': Consumer desire and the social drama of eBay. *Journal of Consumer Culture*, Vol. 10, pp. 56–79.

Dobers, P., and Strannegård, L. (2005), Design, lifestyles and sustainability: Aesthetic consumption in a world of abundance. *Business Strategy and the Environment*, Vol. 14 No. 5, pp. 324–36.

Dolan, P. (2002), The sustainability of 'sustainable consumption'. *Journal of Macromarketing*, Vol. 22 No. 2, pp. 170–81.

Duhachek, A. (2005), Coping: A multidimensional, hierarchical framework of responses to stressful consumption episodes. *Journal of Consumer Research*, Vol. 32 No. 1, pp. 41–53.

EEA. (2012), *Consumption and the Environment – 2012 Update Copenhagen*, European Environmental Agency: 70.

Elliott, R. (1997), Existential consumption and irrational desire. *European Journal of Marketing*, Vol. 31 No. 3/4, pp. 285–96.

Elliott, R. (2004), "Making up people: Consumption as a symbolic vocabulary for the construction of identity", in Ekström, K. and Brembeck, H. (eds.), *Elusive Consumption*, Berg Publishers, Oxford, pp. 11–25.

Erdem, T., Keane, M.P., and Sun, B. (2008), A dynamic model of brand choice when price and advertising signal product quality. *Marketing Science*, Vol. 27 No. 6, pp. 1111–25.

Fuentes, M. (2011), *Att göra hem – en studie av unga mäns boende och konsumtion på 2000-talet*, BAS förlag, Göteborgs universitet, Gothenburg.

Grewal, D., Monroe, K.B., and Krishnan, R. (1998), The effects of price-comparison advertising on buyers' perceptions of acquisition value, transaction value, and behavioral intentions. *Journal of Marketing*, Vol. 62 No. 2.

Holahan, C.J., and Moos, R.H. (1987), Personal and contextual determinants of coping strategies. *Journal of Personality and Social Psychology*, Vol. 52 No. 5, pp. 946–55.

Jantzen, C., Fichett, J., Ostergaard, P., and Vetner, M. (2012), Just for fun? The emotional regime of experiential consumption. *Marketing Theory*, Vol. 12 No. 2, pp. 137–54.

Joy, A., Sherry, J.F., Venkatesh, A., Wang, J., and Chan, R. (2012), Fast fashion, sustainability, and the ethical appeal of luxury brands. *Fashion Theory: The Journal of Dress, Body & Culture*, Vol. 16 No. 3, pp. 273–96.

Kadirov, D., and Varey, R.J. (2013), Neo-structuralist analysis of green-marketing discourse: Interpreting hybrid car manufacturers and consumers. *Consumption Markets & Culture*, Vol. 16 No. 3, pp. 266–89.

Kasser, T. (2002), *The High Price of Materialism*, MIT Press, Cambridge, MA.

Lazarus, R.S., and Folkman, S. (1984), *Stress, Appraisal, and Coping*, Springer Publishing Company, New York.

Markkula, A., and Moisander, J. (2012), Discursive confusion over sustainable consumption: A discursive perspective on the perplexity of marketplace knowledge. *Journal of Consumer Policy*, Vol. 35 No. 1, pp. 105–25.

Moisander, J., Markkula, A., and Eräranta, K. (2010), Construction of consumer choice in the market: Challenges for environmental policy. *International Journal of Consumer Studies*, Vol. 34 No. 1, pp. 73–9.

Mont, O., Heiskanen, E., Power, K., and Kuusi, H. (2013), *Improving Nordic Policymaking By Dispelling Myths on Sustainable Consumption*, Nordic Council of Ministers.

Mont, O., and Plepys, A. (2008), Sustainable consumption progress: Should we be proud or alarmed? *Journal of Cleaner Production*, Vol. 16 No. 4, pp. 531–7.

Morgan, N., Pritchard, A., and Pride, R. (2011), *Destination Brands: Managing Place Reputation*, Routledge, London.

Moschis, G.P. (2007), Stress and consumer behavior. *Journal of the Academy of Marketing Science*, Vol. 35 No. 3, pp. 430–44.

Noguti, V., and Bokeyar, A.L. (2014), Who am I? The relationship between self-concept uncertainty and materialism. *International Journal of Psychology: Journal International de Psychologie*, Vol. 49 No. 5, pp. 323–33.

Platt, R., and Retallack, S. (2009). Consumer power-how the public thinks lower-carbon behaviour could be made mainstream, www.ippr.org/publications/consumer-powerhow-the-public-thinks-lower-carbon-behaviour-could-be-made-mainstream.

Prothero, A., and Fitchett, J.A. (2000), Greening capitalism: Opportunities for a green commodity. *Journal of Macromarketing*, Vol. 20 No. 1, pp. 46–55.

Prothero, A., McDonagh, P., and Dobscha, S. (2010), Is green the new black? Reflections on a green commodity discourse. *Journal of Macromarketing*, Vol. 30 No. 2, pp. 147–59.

Rafferty, K. (2011), Class-based emotions and the allure of fashion consumption. *Journal of Consumer Culture*, Vol. 11 No. 2, pp. 239–60.

Rose, N. (1999), *Powers of Freedom: Reframing Political Thought*. Cambridge University Press, Cambridge.

Sapolsky, R.M. (2004), *Why Zebras Don't Get Ulcers: The Acclaimed Guide to Stress, Stress-Related Diseases, and Coping – Now Revised and Updated*, Macmillan, New York.

Schroeder, J.E., and Zwick, D. (2004), Mirrors of masculinity: Representation and identity in advertising images. *Consumption Markets & Culture*, Vol. 7 No. 1, pp. 21–52.

Shankar, A., Cherrier, H., and Canniford, R. (2006), Consumer empowerment: A Foucauldian interpretation. *European Journal of Marketing*, Vol. 40 No. 9/10, pp. 1013–30.

Shrum, L.J., Lowrey, T.M., Pandelaere, M., Ruvio, A.A., Gentina, E., Furchheim, P., . . . and Steinfield, L. (2014), Materialism: The good, the bad, and the ugly. *Journal of Marketing Management*, Vol. 30 No. 17–18, pp. 1858–81.

Soper, K. (2007), Re-thinking the good life: The citizenship dimension of consumer disaffection with consumerism. *Journal of Consumer Culture*, Vol. 7 No. 2, pp. 205–29.

Southerton, D., Warde, A., *stainable Consumption: The Implications of Changing Infrastructures of Provision*, Edward Elgar Publishing, Cheltenham, UK, pp. 32–48.

Thoits, P.A. (1995), Stress, coping, and social support processes: Where are we? What next? *Journal of Health and Social Behavior*, Vol. 35, pp. 53–79.

Wang, J., and Wallendorf, M. (2006), Materialism, status signaling, and product satisfaction. *Journal of the Academy of Marketing Science*, Vol. 34 No. 4, pp. 494–505.

Zeithaml, V.A. (1988), Consumer perceptions of price, quality, and value: A means-end model and synthesis of evidence. *The Journal of Marketing*, pp. 2–22.

Zwick, D., Bonsu, S.K., and Darmody, A. (2008), Putting consumers to work: 'Co-creation' and new marketing govern-mentality. *Journal of Consumer Culture*, Vol. 8 No. 2, pp. 163–96.

Zwick, D., and Cayla, J. (2011), *Inside Marketing: Practices, Ideologies, Devices*, Oxford University Press, Oxford.

9   Affluent consumer stress and coping in relation to well-being

Literature on compensatory consumption and materialism presented in Chapter 7 indicates that affluent consumption to various extents is motivated by avoiding feeling bad. The self-sustaining and stress-informed spiral of affluent consumption in Figure 8.1 thus has bearing on literature on consumer well-being. Research on consumption and stress confirms that marketplace stressors and consumers' coping strategies can be expected to exert a major influence on well-being (Moschis, 2007). Medical science studies of the relationship between stress, coping and health have indicated that inability to handle stress leads to health problems and mental disorders (Tausig, 1982; Thoits, 1995). Well-being literature distinguishes between objective and subjective measures of well-being. Objective measures are indicators or inputs to well-being that exist independently of the experiencing subject (Veenhoven, 2002). Examples of such objective indicators of well-being are material indicators of standard of living that can be assessed by others than the subject experiencing them. Subjective measures of well-being, on the other hand, are self-reported perceptions of experience. In the literature, subjective measures are commonly recognized as a more comprehensive way to assess well-being (Knight and Rosa, 2011; Veenhoven, 2002). From an embodied stress perspective, where experience is the outcome of the connection between the body and its life-world (Merleau-Ponty, 1962), subjective measures of well-being represent a more trustworthy source of well-being information.

The link between income/consumption and subjective well-being

Literature on subjective well-being (SWB) deals with the weak effect of income (and consumption as it follows disposable income – see Chapter 1) on well-being above certain levels of wealth (Diener et al., 2010; Kahneman and Deaton, 2010; Kahneman et al., 2006; Reisch et al., 2016). The links between SWB and income/consumption level have received significant attention in sustainable consumption literature (Andersson et al., 2014; Jackson, 2005; Knight and Rosa, 2011; Reisch et al., 2016; Wingate et al., 2014).

The SWB body of literature suggests three explanations for the weak link between income and SWB. Reisch et al. observe that "the apparent paradoxes of our current system of consumption and production is that above a certain wealth level, subjective well-being ceases to increase" (2016, p. 236). The first explanation is related to the relative income hypothesis, which claims that it is the relative income of individuals, rather than their absolute income, that has implications for well-being (Dusenberry, 1949; Easterlin, 2001; Frank, 1999; Ferrer-i-Carbonell, 2005). The second, which is closely related to that of relative income, labelled a comparative perspective (Ahuvia and Friedman, 1998), deals with adaption to material standards and individualized norms. The main argument is that as material standards and incomes rise, the criteria for success in terms of material wealth and income increase as well (Csikszentmihalyi, 1999; Easterlin, 1974). The third explanation focuses on sources of happiness, as "nobody has ever claimed that material rewards alone are sufficient to make us happy" (Csikszentmihalyi, 1999, p. 823). Material goods do not fulfil intrinsic human needs, but other conditions, such as close relationships and autonomy, are directly related to individual well-being (Kasser and Ryan, 1993; Myers and Diener, 1995; Ryan and Deci, 2000). Certain basic psychological needs, such as being able to use one's skills, feeling respected and having others to trust, must be fulfilled for us to feel happy (Ryan and Deci, 2000). Pretty et al. (2016) suggest an interesting fourth explanation for the diminishing increases in SWB in affluent economies – the negative side effects of material consumption. Pretty et al. (2016) acknowledge that material consumption increases SWB (Wingate et al., 2014), but at the same time negative externalities erode the SWB effects of such consumption. Examples of such externalities are food, physical activities, healthy minds and community and family links.

One intriguing implication of the SWB/income literature is reported high levels of well-being at modest income levels in studies comparing GDP per capita and SWB in different countries (Pretty, 2013; Reisch et al., 2016; Wingate et al., 2014). Within the so-called double dividend discourse (see Wingate et al., 2014 for a review), data on steadily increased incomes in affluent economies, paired with stable or reduced levels of SWB, have been used as an (inversed) argument that reduced income/consumption levels will increase SWB (Reisch et al., 2016; Wingate et al., 2014). Based on this line of reasoning, sustainable consumption scholars have argued for a double dividend, as decreased consumption will have positive benefits both for our happiness and for the environment in terms of reduced eco-logical footprints (Jackson, 2005). The double dividend line of argument can be contested from an embodied stress perspective. Stress is connected to low SWB and is paralleled by bodily coping (I will elaborate on this later in the section "The dual aspects of subjective well-being"), and therefore stress coping can hide the SWB effects of income. For example, this book suggests that the effects of marketplace stressors, described in Chapters 4 through 6, are in part counterbalanced by learned marketplace stress cop-ing. Thus the stabilizing of SWB over a certain point of GDP per capita, can potentially be explained by stress coping mechanisms used to cope with marketplace stressors. From the stress framework in this book, it follows that (1) increasing affluent income/consumption will entail more marketplace stressors and subsequent consumer stress coping with subsequent negative effects on SWB due to the time and efforts consumers spend on consump-tion for the sake of mood repair and insecurity alleviation, (2) reducing affluent income/consumption will not automatically increase SWB; rather, it will lessen consumers' coping with marketplace stressors and (3) such decreased coping (for the sake of mood repair and insecurity alleviation) might release bodily capacity to engage in activities promoting SWB. Here it is assumed that the gain in SWB is due to consumers' time spent pursu-ing their goals instead of coping with marketplace stressors. Hence from an embodied stress perspective, relatively high SWB in modest income/consumption countries might be explained by more time and energy for activities that make you happy and satisfied and less time spent in the poten-tially stressful marketplace.

Interestingly enough, consumption literature, with the exception of research on compensatory consumption of various sorts – see a detailed overview of the mood-repairing and insecurity-alleviating properties of such consumption in Chapter 7 – to a large degree disregards the well-being effects of afflu-ent consumption. Warde (1994) fails to recognize the emotional well-being effects in his review on consumer choice, consumers' sense of self and the consequences for mental well-being. One of Warde's arguments contests the anxieties of the consumer attitude (Bauman, 1991):

> If self-identity is the paramount value in consumer behaviour, if it is inherently anxiety-provoking, and if the possession and display of material objects is the principal means of handling distress, then it might be anticipated that whole populations of western societies would frequently be in the throes of individual crises. The implication would be a considerable growth of psychiatric problems among the most affluent customers, since they have the most choice of identity.
>
> (Warde, 1994, p. 891)

This chapter contests Warde's position based on research on subjective well-being reviewed from an embodied stress position. The core of the argument in this chapter is based on the stress theory proposition that coping has the capacity to offset the effect of stress. Thus, to the extent that our bodies (including our minds) are affected by marketplace stressors, the effect of such stressors is counterbalanced by bodily coping. In part, therefore, Warde's (1994) reasoning is correct; whole populations of western societies are not in crises. However, from an embodied stress perspective the reason why stressed affluent consumers are not in crises is because they continuously cope with marketplace stressors, and successful coping restores bodily balance.

Subjective well-being and environmental indicators

The concept of Environmental Efficiency of Well-Being (EWEB) is put forward by sustainable consumption scholars to advance knowledge about the links between SWB and consumption-related environmental impacts (Dietz et al., 2009; Knight and Rosa, 2011). This concept includes ecological footprint per capita and average life satisfaction and proposes that "environmental efficiency with which well-being is produced increases with affluence at low to moderate levels of economic development but declines at high levels" (Knight and Rosa, 2011, p. 944). These results are supported by numerous studies on the links between SWB and GHG emissions, in which income is associated with rising GHG emissions and well-being up to a certain high income level where well-being levels off (Lenzen and Cummins, 2013). In a Swedish study on the relationship between GHG emissions and SWB on the individual level using a sample of one thousand respondents, no strong links were found (Andersson et al., 2014). Similar results were found in a Canadian study on GHG emissions from energy from residential use and road transport Wilson et al. (2013). A recent British study on the link between household water consumption and well-being showed no correlation between water use and SWB (Chenoweth et al., 2016).

The link between work hours and subjective well-being

The number of hours spent working in affluent Western countries is negatively related to well-being (Andersson et al., 2014; Kasser and Sheldon, 2009; Pouwels et al., 2008) and positively correlated with environmental pressures (Knight et al., 2013). This work time/SWB relation matches the structural time-related stressors of work rich, time poor affluent consumers discussed in Chapter 6. It is to be expected that affluent consumer time scarcity that has an impact on consumer chronic role strains affects SWB. As noted in Chapter 6, research clearly indicates that activities missed out because of long working hours, e.g. time with children, socializing with friends, sleeping etc., are more important for SWB than the consumption enabled by the income gained by working longer hours (Holmberg and Nässén, 2010).

The dual aspects of subjective well-being: implications of an embodied stress perspective

The links between SWB on the one hand and income/consumption, GHG emissions or working hours on the other can purposefully be problematized by recognizing the dual aspects of SWB, emotional well-being and life evaluation (Diener et al., 2010; Kahneman and Deaton, 2010). Emotional well-being refers to feelings like joy, fascination, anxiety, sadness, etc. and life evaluation to thought content about one's life. Life evaluation is most commonly quantitatively measured by asking "How satisfied are you with your life as a whole these days?" and respondents are asked to rate his or her life on a scale where 0 is "the worst possible life for you" and 10 is "the best possible life for you" (Kahneman and Deaton, 2010, p. 1). Emotional well-being is assessed by questions about the presence of various emotions (enjoyment, happiness, anger, sadness, stress, worry) the day before answering the questionnaire. In their study, Kahneman and Deaton observed differences in the relationship of the emotional and the cognitive aspects (life evaluation) of well-being to income (2010).

In Kahneman and Deaton's study emotional well-being was measured as positive affect (smiling, enjoyment and happiness), blue affect (sadness and worry) and stress. The results show that for all measures of emotional well-being "beyond about \$75,000/y, there is no improvement whatever in any of the three measures of emotional well-being". In contrast, "the effects of income on individuals' life evaluations show no satiation, at least to an amount well over \$120,000" (Kahneman and Deaton, 2010, p. 3). These findings – income (and thus consumption) is positively related to cognitive life evaluation but not to positive feelings such as happiness – can be understood from an embodied stress framework. Following these results affluent consumption is not connected to positive emotions in general, but rather to positive cognitive evaluation of one's standard of living in relation to that of others. This makes perfect sense from an embodied stress perspective in which affluent consumption in the Western consumer culture context is proposed to be accompanied by marketplace stressors, which entail negative emotions as frustration, anxiety and loss of control. When coped with through support-seeking coping (consumption of the socially desirable), it will affect the evaluation of life, as this coping-incentivized consumption is highly affected by social norms and acceptance.

Mood repair as one important motivator of affluent Western consumption seems to contradict the idea that such consumption does not make us happier. In the same vein as earlier, we can argue that from an embodied stress perspective, affluent marketplace environmental, internalized and structural stressors – which cause insecurity, anxiety, confusion, overload, frustration, "think ideal, feel bad" sequences etc. – are likely to decrease emotional well-being. Coping with such stress by means of consuming socially desirable products endorsed by peers and experts (support-seeking coping) takes on insecurity-alleviating qualities which most probably increase the cognitive evaluation of one's life, but not necessarily how one feels.

In sum, research evidence of affluent marketplace stressors and consumers' stress coping strategies (support-seeking coping based on continuous consumption), illustrated as a spiral (Figure 8.1 in Chapter 8) in this book, feeds well into research findings that conclude that income/consumption do not always correlate positively with SWB. Rather, affluent consumption is related to *both* increased SWB – increased life evaluation when feeling happy when the latest and highly socially desirable model of smart phone is purchased – and reduced emotional well-being when yet another new model of smartphone is launched on the market which makes the older version seem outdated, socially not desirable and perceived as a potential social threat. The embodied stress framework presented in this book thus provides a nuanced understanding for the link between income/consumption and SWB.

SWB, stress and mental ill health

From an embodied stress perspective, links between income/consumption and SWB potentially have implications on mental health. In a review on literature on SWB, health and longevity, it is concluded that SWB, in particular emotional well-being, predicts health in healthy populations (Diener and Chan, 2011).

> In sum, moods and emotions are consistently found to be associated with biological measures such as blood pressure, cortisol, and inflammation, as well as indicators of disease such as artery wall thickening. Importantly, the relation of positive feelings with physiology occurs in addition to the effects of negative feelings and depression, suggesting that positive affect may have distinctive biological correlates that can benefit health.
>
> (Diener and Chan, 2011, p. 14)

High blood pressure, elevated levels of cortisol, reduced functioning of the immune system and cardiovascular diseases are well-known physical effects of chronic stress (Währborg, 2002). Moods and emotions are particularly associated with cardiovascular disease (Steptoe et al., 2007), and SWB as negative affect (e.g. stress, anxiety, depression) is related to both detrimental cardiovascular changes and the functioning of the immune system (Howell et al., 2007). Studies focusing on time stress and SWB as emotional well-being suggest that (Gärling et al., 2014, 2016; Ng et al., 2009) time stress seriously affects family life, progress in working life and various leisure goals and thus has a negative impact on emotional well-being. Time stress is seen as an impediment to goal progress in life. Such goal progress is stipulated to increase emotional well-being (Klug and Maier, 2015). The negative relation between time stress and mental health is confirmed by Frankenhaeuser et al. (1989) who observed increased norepinephrine (a stress hormone) levels in women who experienced the double burden of having the main responsibility for the family and of work.

Possible externalities of affluent consumption particularly relevant from a stress perspective are high levels of mental ill health among affluent consumers in Western consumer cultures (Pretty et al., 2016). The prevalence of mental ill health in affluent economies and the connection between mental health, income and stress is confirmed by the Roadmap for Mental Health Research in Europe (ROAMER), a three-year project funded by the European Commission under the Seventh Framework Programme. ROAMER states "the already high burden and impact of mental disorders throughout Europe (WHO, 2001) is expected to rise, partly because of the aging phenomena, and partly because of unabated social and economic stressors contributing to depression and anxiety disorders" (ROAMER, 2017). Empirical studies on the prevalence of mental illness in developed economies (USA, France, Netherlands, Belgium, Spain, Germany, Italy and Japan) show strong positive linear associations between gross national income (GNI) per capita and mental illness (Pickett et al., 2006). *Within* these countries, socioeconomic disadvantages such as low education, unemployment, low levels of social capital etc., are related to mental illness. Thus, it seems that mental illness is related both to income levels and to income inequality (Pickett et al., 2006; Reiss, 2013). To provide knowledge about the putative intricate relationships between stress, mental health and income/consumption is outside the scope of this book, which merely aims to suggest that these relationships are under-researched.

Sweden can serve as example of the need for understanding complex connections between affluent consumption, the dual dimensions of SWB, stress and mental illness. Sweden is ranked as one of the richest countries in the world. With a GNI per capita of 57.900 US dollars in 2015, Sweden is ranked

14 among the countries in the world by the World Bank (2017). In 2013, emotional well-being was measured as the frequency of being happy in the last four weeks. In a sample of Swedes, 15% considered themselves happy always, 53% considered themselves happy most of the time, 24% sometimes, 5% rarely and 3% answered they are never happy (Eurostat, 2017). The same year (2013), average life satisfaction among Swedes was 8.0 on a 1–10 scale (Eurostat, 2017). Almost the same results are found on rank lists of Happiness in nations 2005–2014 (Veenhoven, World Database of Happiness, 2017). On a 1–10 scale, the average Swede answers the survey question "Taking all together, how satisfied or dissatisfied are you with your life-as-a-whole these days?" with 7.8 (compared with 8.5 for Costa Rica and 2.5 for Tanzania).

For mental health in Sweden, The Public Health Agency of Sweden (2017) reports that

> Over the last decade the proportion of persons in Sweden with problems of nervousness, apprehension or anxiety has been relatively unchanged among 16–84-year-olds. In the age group 16–29 years, the proportion with this type of problem was 54 percent among women and 33 percent among men in 2016. In the other age groups, the figure is roughly one-third for women and one-fourth for men. Since the mid-1980s, self-reported mental and somatic problems have increased among school children in Sweden, primarily among 13 and 15-year-old girls.

Stress was the most common reason for mental ill health in Sweden in 2015, and stress-related illness represented 14% of ill health this year (Försäkringskassan, 2015). Swedish statistics on reasons for absence from work due to illness 2013–2015 show dramatic changes. There was a reported 73% increase in stress-related sick-leaves during this period of time (Dagens Nyheter, 2015). In Sweden, stress-related diagnoses are most common among working women aged 30–39 years who carry the responsibility for children and the home.

The example of Sweden shows a great need for scientific investigations of the relationship between affluent consumption, SWB and stress. The relationship between emotional well-being and average life evaluation for Sweden corresponds with SWB literature in which emotional well-being returns are stipulated to diminish with increased levels of wealth. Life evaluation at 8.0 on average seems to be in line with proposed linear relations between wealth and life satisfaction. However, the great disparity between average life evaluations of 8.0 and 68% of Swedes being self-reported as always happy or happy most of the time (Eurostat, 2017), and increasing levels of stress-related illness in Sweden, is not only a matter of great concern but also a call to scientifically address the links between stress, SWB and affluent consumption. Maybe the Swedes that stated that they were happy sometimes (24%), rarely (5%) or never (3%) can inform us as to why, in one of the most affluent countries in the world, stress-related illness is a growing problem. This book suggests that part of the answer to this question is to be found in the affluent marketplace.

Bibliography

Ahuvia, A.C., and Friedman, D.C. (1998), Income, consumption, and subjective well-being: Toward a composite macromarketing model. *Journal of Macromarketing*, Vol. 18 No. 2, pp. 153–68.

Andersson, D., Nässén, J., and Larsson, J. (2014), Greenhouse gas emissions and subjective well-being: An analysis of Swedish households. *Ecological Economics*, Vol. 102, pp. 75–82.

Bauman, Z. (1991), *Thinking Sociologically*, Blackwell, Cambridge, MA.

Chenoweth, J., López-Avilés, A., Morse, S., and Druckman, A. (2016), Water consumption and subjective wellbeing: An analysis of British households. *Ecological Economics*, Vol. 130, pp. 186–94.

Csikszentmihalyi, M. (1999), If we are so rich, why aren't we happy? *American Psychologist*, Vol. 54 No. 10, pp. 821–7.

Dagens Nyheter. (2015), Dramatic increase in stress-related sick leave, www.dn.se/ekonomi/dramatisk-okning-av-stressrelaterade-sjukskrivningar/

Diener, E., and Chan, M.Y. (2011), Happy people live longer: Subjective well-being contributes to health and longevity. *Applied Psychology: Health and Well-Being*, Vol. 3 No. 1, pp. 1–43.

Diener, E., Ng, W., Harter, J., and Arora, R. (2010), Wealth and happiness across the world: Material prosperity predicts life evaluation, whereas psychosocial prosperity predicts positive feeling. *Journal of Personality and Social Psychology*, Vol. 99 No. 1, pp. 52–61.

Dietz, T., Rosa, E.A., and York, R. (2009), Environmentally efficient well-being: Rethinking sustainability as the relationship between human well-being and environmental impacts. *Human Ecology Review*, Vol. 16 No. 1, pp. 114–23.

Dolan, P., Peasgood, T., and White, M. (2008), Do we really know what makes us happy? A review of the economic literature on the factors associated with subjective well-being. *Journal of Economic Psychology*, Vol. 29 No. 1, pp. 94–122.

Dusenberry, J. (1949), *Income, Saving and the Theory of Consumer Behaviour*, Harvard University Press, Cambridge, MA.

Easterlin, R.A. (1974), "Does economic growth improve the human lot? Some empirical evidence", in David, P. and Reder, M. (eds.), *Nations and Households in Economic Growth, Essays in Honor of Moses Abramowitz*, Academic Press, New York, pp. 89–125.

Easterlin, R.A. (2001), Income and happiness: Towards a unified theory. *The Economic Journal*, Vol. 111 No. 473, pp. 465–84.

Eurostat (2017), Quality of life in Europe, http://ec.europa.eu/eurostat/statistics-explained/index.php/Quality_of_life_in_Europe_-_facts_and_views_-_overall_life_satisfaction

Ferrer-i-Carbonell, A. (2005), Income and well-being: An empirical analysis of the comparison income effect. *Journal of Public Economics*, Vol. 89, pp. 997–1019.

Försäkringskassan. (2015), Stress commonest cause of sick leave, www.forsakringskassan.se/press/pressmeddelanden/

Frank, R. (1999), *Luxury Fever*, Princeton University Press, Princeton.

Frankenhaeuser, M., Lundberg, U., Fredrikson, M., Melin, B., Tuomisto, M., Myrsten, A.-L., et al. (1989), Stress on and off the job as related to sex and occupational status in white-collar workers. *Journal of Organizational Behavior*, Vol. 10, pp. 321–46. doi:10.1002/job.4030100404.

Gärling, T., Gamble, A., Fors, F., and Hjerm, M. (2016), Emotional well-being related to time pressure, impediment to goal progress, and stress-related symptoms. *Journal of Happiness Studies*, Vol. 17 No. 5, pp. 1789–99.

Gärling, T., Krause, K., Gamble, A., and Hartig, T. (2014), Time pressure and emotional well-being. *PsyCH Journal*, Vol. 3, pp. 132–43. doi:10.1002/pchj.52.

Holmberg, J., and Nässén, J. (2010), Well-being the path out of the consumption – Climate dilemma? *Beyond the Consumption Bubble*, Vol. 221.

Howell, R.T., Kern, M.L., and Lyubomirsky, S. (2007), Health benefits: Metaanalytically determining the impact of well-being on objective health outcomes. *Health Psychology Review*, Vol. 1, pp. 83–136.

Jackson, T. (2005), Live better by consuming less?: Is there a 'double dividend' in sustainable consumption? *Journal of Industrial Ecology*, Vol. 9 No. 1–2, pp. 19–36.

Kahneman, D., and Deaton, A. (2010), High income improves evaluation of life but not emotional well-being. *PNAS*, Vol. 127 No. 38, pp. 16489–93.

Kahneman, D., Kruegers, A., Schakade, D., Schwartz, N., and Stone, A. (2006), Would you be happier if you were richer? *Science*, Vol. 312, pp. 1908–10.

Kasser, T., and Ryan, R.M. (1993), A dark side of the American dream: Correlates of financial success as a central life aspiration. *Journal of Personality and Social Psychology*, Vol. 65, pp. 410–22.

Kasser, T., and Sheldon, K.M. (2009), Time affluence as a path toward personal happiness and ethical business practice: Empirical evidence from four studies. *Journal of Business Ethics*, Vol. 84 No. 2, pp. 243–55.

Klug, H.J., and Maier, G.W. (2015), Linking goal progress and subjective well-being: A meta-analysis. *Journal of Happiness Studies*, Vol. 16 No. 1, pp. 37–65.

Knight, K.W., and Rosa, E.A. (2011), The environmental efficiency of well-being: A cross-national analysis. *Social Science Research*, Vol. 40, pp. 931–49.

Knight, K.W., Rosa, E.A., and Schor, J.B. (2013), Could working less reduce pressures on the environment? A cross-national panel analysis of OECD countries, 1970–2007. *Global Environmental Change*, Vol. 23 No. 4, pp. 691–700.

Kuppens, P., Realo, A., and Diener, E. (2008), The role of positive and negative emotions in life satisfaction judgment across nations. *Journal of Personality and Social Psychology*, Vol. 95 No. 1, p. 66.

Lenzen, M., and Cummins, R.A. (2013), Happiness versus the environment – A case study of Australian lifestyles. *Challenges*, Vol. 4 No. 1, pp. 56–74.

Merleau-Ponty, M. (1962), *Phenomenology of Perception*, Routledge, London.

Moschis, G. (2007), Stress and consumer behaviour. *Journal of the Academy of Marketing Science*, Vol. 35, pp. 430–44.

Myers, D.G., and Diener, E. (1995), Who is happy. *Psychological Science*, Vol. 6, pp. 10–19.

Ng, W., Diener, E., Arora, R., and Harter, J. (2009), Affluence, feelings of stress, and well-being. *Social Indicators Research*, Vol. 94, pp. 257–71. doi:10.1007/s11205-008-9422-5.

Pavot, W., and Diener, E. (2008), The satisfaction with life scale and the emerging construct of life satisfaction. *The Journal of Positive Psychology*, Vol. 3 No. 2, pp. 137–52.

Pickett, K.E., James, O.W., and Wilkinson, R.G. (2006), Income inequality and the prevalence of mental illness: A preliminary international analysis. *Journal of Epidemiology and Community Health*, Vol. 60 No. 7, pp. 646–7.

Pouwels, B., Siegers, J., and Vlasblom, J.D. (2008), Income, working hours, and happiness. *Economics Letters*, Vol. 99 No. 1, pp. 72–4.

Pretty, J. (2013), The consumption of a finite planet: Well-being, convergence, divergence and the nascent green economy. *Environmental & Resource Economics*, Vol. 55, pp. 475–99.

Pretty, J. et al. (2016), Improving health and well-being independently of GDP: Dividends of greener and prosocial economies. *International Journal of Environ Mental Health Research*, Vol. 26 No. 1, pp. 11–36.

The Public Health Agency of Sweden. (2017), Impaired mental wellbeing, www.folkhalsomyndigheten.se/folkhalsorapportering-statistik/folkhalsans-utveckling/halsa/psykisk-ohalsa/nedsatt-psykiskt-valbefinnande/

Reisch, L.A., Cohen, M.J., Thøgersen, J.B., and Tukker, A. (2016), Frontiers in sustainable consumption research. *GAIA-Ecological Perspectives for Science and Society*, Vol. 25 No. 4, pp. 234–40.

Reiss, F. (2013), Socioeconomic inequalities and mental health problems in children and adolescents: A systematic review. *Social Science & Medicine*, Vol. 90, pp. 24–31.

ROAMER. (2017), *Background Information*, www.roamer-mh.org/index.php?page=1_3, accessed May 28, 2017.

Ryan, R.M., and Deci, E.L. (2000), Self-determination theory and the facilitation of intrinsic motivation, social development, and well-being. *American Psychologist*, Vol. 55, pp. 68–78.

Steptoe, A., O'Donnell, K., Badrick, E., Kumari, M., and Marmot, M. (2007), Neuroendocrine and inflammatory factors associated with positive affect in healthy men and women. *American Journal of Epidemiology*, Vol. 167, pp. 96–102.

Tausig, M. (1982), Measuring life events. *Journal of Health and Social Behaviour*, Vol. 23, pp. 52–64.

Thoits, P.A. (1995), Stress, coping, and social support processes: Where are we? What next? *Journal of Health and Social Behavior*, Vol. 35, pp. 53–79.

Veenhoven, R. (2002), Why social policy needs subjective indicators. *Social Indicators Research*, Vol. 58 No. 1–3, pp. 33–46.

Veenhoven, R. (2007), "Subjective measures of well-being", in McGillivray, M. (ed.), *Human Well-Being*, Palgrave Macmillan, London, pp. 214–39.

Veenhoven, R. (2017), *Happiness in Sweden (SE)*, World Database of Happiness, Erasmus University Rotterdam, The Netherlands, http://worlddatabaseofhappiness. eur.nl, accessed May 30, 2017.

Währborg, P. (2002), *Stress och den nya ohälsan*, Natur och kultur, Stockholm.

Warde, A. (1994), Consumption, identity-formation and uncertainty. *Sociology*, Vol. 28 No. 4, pp. 877–98.

Wilson, J., Tyedmers, P., and Spinney, J.E. (2013), An exploration of the relationship between socioeconomic and well-being variables and household greenhouse gas emissions. *Journal of Industrial Ecology*, Vol. 17 No. 6, pp. 880–91.

Wingate, D., Middlemiss, L., and Wesselink, A. (2014), *The 'double dividend' discourse in sustainable consumption: Happiness, human nature, and the reproduction of economic doctrine*, Sustainability Research Institute Paper, University of Leeds, Leeds.

World Bank. *World Development Indicators Database*, http://databank.worldbank. org/data/download/GNIPC.pdf, accessed 28 April 2017.

World Health Organization. (2001), *The World Health Report 2001. Mental Health: New Understanding, New Hope*, World Health Organization, Geneva.

10 Promoting affluent sustainable consumption from a stress perspective
A theoretical outlook

From an embodied perspective, affluent consumption is largely promoted by marketplace actors. In line with the idea of the intentional arc (Merleau-Ponty, 1962), consumers' experiences of the practices undertaken by market actors in the marketplace become embodied (sedimented in the body, including the mind) in terms of pre-reflective bodily perceptive skills to understand the marketplace. The concept of affordances (Gibson, 1979) can help us understand that consumers thus become disposed to respond to the solicitations of marketplace offerings and that consumers' perceptions of market offerings "afford" certain actions (Dreyfus, 2002). Thus from an embodied stress perspective, the promotion of affluent sustainable consumption must include all actors that have an impact on the marketplace.

The embodied view on consumption represented by this book shares many similarities with the socio-material understanding of consumption in constructivist market studies (e.g. Araujo, 2007; Kjellberg and Helgesson, 2006, 2007). Within this literature informed by economic sociology, two types of configurative elements are identified: *market practices*, i.e. the interaction between market actors in a market configuration, and *market actors*, who take part in market practices (Araujo et al., 2008; Storbacka and Nenonen, 2011). The market practice literature suggests that markets, as socio-material networks, can be conceptualized as being constituted by three interlinked "dense areas of activity" (Kjellberg and Helgesson, 2007, p. 145): exchange practices, representational practices and normalizing practices (Kjellberg and Helgesson, 2007). Market practices are defined as "all activities that contribute to constitute markets" (Kjellberg and Helgesson, 2006, p. 842). Thus, various market actors (including firms, consumers, NGOs, government agencies etc.) affect individual consumers and their choices of products and services through their market practices (Geiger et al., 2014; Cochoy, 2008). The notions of consumer agency, agencement or agencing are used to signify consumers' capacity to shape markets (Harrison and Kjellberg, 2016; Stigzelius, 2017). These concepts entail an understanding for consumption as collectively created by networks of humans and material entities (Callon, 2007, 2008; Cochoy et al., 2016; Latour, 2005). Hence, consumption is seen as a collectively created phenomena and consumers are seen as both produced by and producing markets (Stigzelius, 2017). Such a view is in alignment with an embodied view on consumption that recognizes that consumer bodies respond to the solicitations of the marketplace and that consumer bodies partake in the experience of this marketplace.

The market constructivist understanding of consumption is instrumental in efforts to change, or shape, market configurations in any specific direction. Efforts to promote affluent sustainable consumption accompanied with, or enabled by, less chronic consumer role strains could potentially build on socio-material theories of consumer capacity to act as a result of different socio-material arrangements in actor-networks. These collectively produce specific agencements, which are defined as " 'arrangements endowed with the capacity of acting in different ways depending on their configuration' (Callon, 2007, p. 320). From this line of reasoning, it follows that (1) affluent consumers' capacity to consume in a sustainable manner is shaped by marketing practices, and (2) marketing practice frames consumer experiences of the marketplace as stressful.

Examples of how marketing practice shapes affluent consumption are, as previously discussed, related to pricing, assortment, advertising, arranging products in stores, government policies which regulate these market actors through taxes and regulations, sustainability certifications schemes etc. (Geiger et al., 2014; Markkula and Moisander, 2012). Branding, advertising and product replacement and renewal are examples of marketing practices that suggest consumption based desired life-styles compatible with specific brands (Arvidsson, 2005; Caruana and Crane, 2008; Zwick et al., 2008). The mechanism by which such marketing practices partake in the configuring of markets, and thus the shaping of consumers' capacity to act, is the translations between exchange practices (activities making economic exchange possible), representational practices (activities producing images of markets, bridging distances in time and between market actors) and normalizing practices (activities establishing objectives for how a market should work according to certain market actors) (Kjellberg and Helgesson, 2007). As an example, fashion branding contributes to the configuration of the fashion market through influencing exchange, representational and normalizing practices (Solér et al., 2015). Fashion brand discourse shapes exchange practices (making economic exchange possible) by stabilising the object of exchange (as a brand) through various promotional activities, such as advertising and in-store displays. Fashion brand discourse has a huge impact on representational practices by suggesting fashion identity-related meanings (what it means to be a fashion consumer, what the fashion consumer needs in terms of novel products and what price the fashion consumer is willing to pay for clothing). Hence, fashion brand discourse contributes strongly to normalizing practices by suggesting normative objectives valid for the fashion market in terms of guidelines on how the fashion market should work according to some market actors or group of market actors.

Market studies literature can guide initiatives on how marketing practices can shape the sustainability of affluent consumption and partake in the creation of less stressful marketplaces. Within the field of market studies, studies on concerned markets – i.e. "market configurations that take into account the various concerns that are associated with the unfolding of economic transaction" (Geiger et al., 2014, p. 2) – are particularly valid for this book. Both sustainability and stress are indeed concerns associated with economic transactions in the Western affluent marketplace. Matters of concern are defined as "those things and situations that – for better or for worse – are related to us, can affect us, and worry us" Geiger et al. (2014, p. 2). Now the question is how scientific understandings of concerned markets can guide market practices that shape sustainable and stress-free affluent consumption. Literature suggests that in order for social concerns (such as sustainability and stress) to be activated and incorporated in market discourse and objects, political controversy, debate and negotiation of taken-for-granted assumptions are needed (Callon et al., 2002; Cochoy, 2014). Hence, only when sustainability and stress become a matter of concern that can be valued and priced and affect exchange, representational and normative market practices can we expect market actors to change (Kjellberg and Helgesson, 2007). Azimont and Araujo (2014) show that in the case of the market for functional foods, the health benefits of functional food as a matter of concern were created by first heating up the debate over what functional food is and then cooling down this debate by agreeing on certain characteristics of such food. In this sense, matters of concern are a way to create markets (Azimont and Araujo, 2014; Cochoy, 2014). The opportunity to create sustainable and stress-free affluent marketplaces thus depends on what "power asymmetries between the actors and their ability to marketize concerns and concernize markets" exist and what values are assigned to sustainable and stress-free market practices (Cochoy, 2014, p. 247).

In accordance with an embodied stress perspective, marketplaces in which stressors are reduced will shape consumer bodily perception, skills and behavior attuned to such decreased levels of stress. As discussed and proposed in Chapters 7 and 8 in this book, less stressful marketplaces entail increasing emotional well-being and more sustainable levels of affluent consumption. However, as described in Chapter 8, dominant marketing governmentality techniques seem to stand in sharp contrast to a less stressful affluent marketplace. The possibilities of problem-focused coping to be provided (afforded) by contemporary and current affluent marketplaces are therefore severely limited. Theories on concerned markets provide a promising avenue towards new affluent marketplaces in which the social concerns of stress and sustainability are debated and valued. Scientists, politicians and legislators need to take an active role in the making of these new and concerned marketplaces.

Bibliography

Araujo, L. (2007), Markets, market-making and marketing. *Marketing Theory*, Vol. 7 No. 3, pp. 211–26.

Araujo, L., Kjellberg, H., and Spencer, R. (2008), Market practices and forms: Introduction to the special issue. *Marketing Theory*, Vol. 8 No. 1, pp. 5–14.

Arvidsson, A. (2005), Brands: A critical perspective. *Journal of Consumer Culture*, Vol. 5 No. 2, pp. 235–58.

Azimont, F., and Araujo, L. (2014), Credible qualifications: The case of functional foods. *Concerned Markets: Economic Ordering for Multiple Values*, pp. 46–71.

Callon, M. (2007), "What does it mean to say that economics is performative", in MacKenzie, D., Muniesa, F., and Siu, L. (eds.), *Do Economists Make Markets? On the Performativity of Economics*, Princeton University Press, Princeton, pp. 311–57.

Callon, M. (2008), "Economic markets and the rise of interactive agencements: From prosthetic agencies to habilitated agencies", in Pinch, T. and Swedberg, R. (eds.), *Living in a Material World: Economic Sociology Meets Science and Technology Studies*, MIT Press, Cambridge, MA, pp. 29–56.

Callon, M., Méadel, C., and Rabeharisoa, V. (2002), The economy of qualities. *Economy and Society*, Vol. 31 No. 2, pp. 194–217.

Caruana, R., and Crane, A. (2008), Constructing consumer responsibility: Exploring the role of corporate communications. *Organization Studies*, Vol. 29 No. 12, pp. 1495–519.

Cochoy, F. (2008), Calculation, qualculation, calqulation: Shopping cart arithmetic, equipped cognition and the clustered consumer. *Marketing Theory*, Vol. 8 No. 15, pp. 15–44.

Cochoy, F. (2014), Concerned markets: Facing the future, beyond 'interested' and 'contested' markets. *Concerned Markets: Economic Ordering for Multiple Values*, Vol. 238.

Cochoy, F., Trompette, P., and Araujo, L. (2016), From market agencements to market agencing: An introduction. *Consumption Markets & Culture*.

Dreyfus, H.L. (2002), Intelligence without representation – Merleau-Ponty's critique of mental representation the relevance of phenomenology to scientific explanation. *Phenomenology and the Cognitive Sciences*, Vol. 1 No. 4, pp. 367–83.

Geiger, S., Harrison, D., Kjellberg, H., and Mallard, A. (eds.). (2014), *Concerned Markets: Economic Ordering for Multiple Values*, Edward Elgar, Cheltenham, UK.

Gibson, J.J. (1979), "The theory of affordances", in *The Ecological Approach to Visual Perception*, Houghton Mifflin Harcourt, Hopewell, pp. 56–60.

Harrison, D., and Kjellberg, H. (2016), How users shape and use markets. *Marketing Theory*, Vol. 16 No. 4, pp. 1–24.

Kjellberg, H., and Helgesson, C.-F. (2006), Multiple versions of markets: Multiplicity and performativity in market practice. *Industrial Marketing Management*, Vol. 35, pp. 839–55.

Kjellberg, H., and Helgesson, C.-F. (2007), On the nature of markets and their practices. *Marketing Theory*, Vol. 7, pp. 137–61.

Latour, B. (2005), *Reassembling the Social – An Introduction to Actor-Network-Theory*, Oxford University Press, Oxford.

Markkula, A., and Moisander, J. (2012), Discursive confusion over sustainable consumption: A discursive perspective on the perplexity of marketplace knowledge. *Journal of Consumer Policy*, Vol. 35 No. 1, pp. 105–25.

Merleau-Ponty, M. (1962), *Phenomenology of Perception*, Routledge, London.

Solér, C., Baeza, J., and Svärd, C. (2015), Construction of silence on issues of sustainability through branding in the fashion market. *Journal of Marketing Management*, Vol. 31 No. 1–2, pp. 219–46.

Stigzelius, I. (2017), *Producing Consumers: Agencing and Concerning Consumers to Do Green in Everyday Food Practices*, Doctoral Thesis, Stockholm School of Economics.

Storbacka, K., and Nenonen, S. (2011), Markets as configurations. *European Journal of Marketing*, Vol. 45 No. 1/2, pp. 241–58.

Zwick, D., Bonsu, S.K., and Darmody, A. (2008), Putting consumers to work: 'Co-creation' and new marketing govern-mentality. *Journal of Consumer Culture*, Vol. 8 No. 2, pp. 163–96.

Index

acceleration of consumption, psychological risks of 71–2
active stress-coping strategies 79
actual identity 56
acute marketplace stressors 32–3
addictive compensatory consumption 61
advertising 97
aesthetic consumption 60
affluence and consumption, sustainability of 6–9; *see also* affluent consumption; sustainable consumption
affluence hypothesis, consequences of 5–6
affluent consumer stress: well-being and, coping in relation to 105–13; *see also* subjective well-being (SWB)
affluent consumption: climate gas emissions and 9; compensatory consumption and, link between 83; defined 4–6, 65; dimensions of 5; in dispersed practice, concept of 72–3; emotion-based identity-making in 80; environmental impact of 4–6, 68–9; fashion consumption and 72–3; financial resources for, enabling of 5; identity-making in, individualized-based 80; interdependent 5; as kinship in practice 54–6; market constructivist understanding of 118; materialism and, reducing of 92, 95; mood-enhancing 84; perceptual overload and, link

between 48; problem-focused coping and 97, 101, 120; socio-material understanding of 117; stress-informed spiral of 95; sustainability and, consequences of 67; time pressure of 71–2; value orientation and 86; well-being and, consequences of 67; Western economies, characteristic of 4–5; *see also* affluent sustainable consumption, specific topics on
affluent marketplace: perceptual overload characteristic of 45; problem-focused coping in 96; support-seeking coping strategy in 83
affluent sustainable consumption: stress perspective, promoting from 25–6, 117–20; from stress perspective, embodiment of 9–13; *see also* affluent consumption; sustainable consumption
affordances, concept of 25, 36–7, 117
agencements 118
allostatic balance 24–5
anxiety: compensatory consumption and 71, 83; consumption, caused by 56, 61; consumption objects and 56; defined 54–5; fashion consumption and 55; identity and, link between 54; insecurity and 86–7; psychological 60; social 60; SWB and 107–8
arousal 33, 44–5
aspirational identity 56
avoidance stress-coping strategies 79

www.ingramcontent.com/pod-product-compliance
Ingram Content Group UK Ltd.
Pitfield, Milton Keynes, MK11 3LW, UK
UKHW020419010325
455677UK00029B/943